SHORT
NATURE
WALKS
ON LONG ISLAND

P9-CQD-373

Praise for previous editions:

"A series of interesting walking tours . . . that require anywhere from a half hour to two hours or more. But there's no hurry, and you can proceed at your own leisurely pace. Happy hiking."
—*Newsday* (Long Island, N.Y.)

"Walks are clearly mapped with details on what to expect from each of the areas visited . . . this book will enhance your explorations [of Long Island]."
—*Country Home/Country Gardens*

Help Us Keep This Guide Up to Date

Every effort has been made by the author and editors to make this guide as accurate and useful as possible. However, many things can change after a guide is published—establishments close, phone numbers change, hiking trails are rerouted, facilities come under new management, etc.

We would love to hear from you concerning your experiences with this guide and how you feel it could be made better and be kept up to date. While we may not be able to respond to all comments and suggestions, we'll take them to heart, and we'll also make certain to share them with the author. Please send your comments and suggestions to the following address:

The Globe Pequot Press
Reader Response/Editorial Department
P.O. Box 480
Guilford, CT 06437

Or you may e-mail us at:

editorial@globe-pequot.com

Thanks for your input, and happy travels!

SHORT NATURE WALKS

ON LONG ISLAND

Seventh Edition

by
Rodney and Priscilla Albright

revised and edited by
Kenneth Kindler

The Globe Pequot Press

Guilford, Connecticut

Photography credits: Pages xviii, 4, and 59, Long Island State Park Commission; page 38, Ward Melville Heritage Organization; page 96, D.E. Tripp; page 154, John Hollingsworth/Department of Interior Fish and Wildlife Service; pages 124 and 170, Robert L. Wendt

Cover photo: Stone Images
Cover design: Lana Mullen
Map credits: Basic data courtesy of Lawrence G. Paul

Library of Congress Cataloging-in-Publication Data

Albright, Rodney.
    Short nature walks on Long Island / by Rodney and Priscilla Albright.—7th ed. / revised and edited by Kenneth Kindler.
        p. cm.
    ISBN 0-7627-0905-7
    1. Hiking—New York (State)—Long Island—Guidebooks.   2. Long Island (N.Y.)—Guidebooks.   I. Albright, Priscilla.   II. Kindler, Kenneth.   III. Title.
GV199.42.N652L662   2001

                                        2001023955

Manufactured in the United States of America
Seventh Edition/First Printing

To The Nature Conservancy

Contents

33 20

49 50 14

17
12 32 40   19
29 30
28   18   23

11   31
Nassau
County   13

Queens
County   38 39   2

37   1

36

16 47
48
53
26 46
27 10
52 45 9
51 15 8
43 25 7
23 44 5 6
42
Suffolk
County 4
24
3

Map Legend

for maps accompanying walk descriptions

· — · · — ·	Preserve Boundary	▲	Viewpoint
────	Major Highway	┼┼┼┼┼┼	Railroad
────	Other Roads	⬤25⬢37	State and County Routes
═══════	Woods Roads	★	Parking Areas
- - - - - -	Trails	Ⓟ	Permit Parking (see page 2)
• • • • • • •	Choice Walks	W	White-Paint Blazes
■ ■ ■ ■ ■ ■	Nassau-Suffolk Greenbelt Trail	🌫	Lakes and Ponds
· + + + + + +	Long Island Greenbelt and Pine Barrens Trails		

Preface to the Seventh Edition

Several years ago a friend of mine asked if I would like to join him on a walk that he thought I might find surprising. We drove to the trailhead and parked by the side of a wooded road. I had driven on this road many times, but had never noticed the entrance to this trail. After walking a short distance we encountered an incredible natural splendor—a panoply of forgotten sights, sounds, and aromas. We reached a coastal plain pond, with water of a deep-blue color, reflecting clouds and luxuriant foliage. As we watched an Osprey rip a fish from the pond, it was hard to believe that we were still on Long Island. We were only a few miles from crowded shopping malls and congested roads, but a short walk had transported us to the serenity and magic of a nearby woodland.

My friend Bill can't take you out there for your first walk, but it is my hope that this very useful guide created by the Albrights and updated by editors who love the island and are active walkers, will encourage you to experience the Natural Island on your own.

Although there has been considerable development on Long Island, there are many groups, agencies, and organizations that are effectively working to protect this island's unique natural habitat. The following list of contacts will be helpful if you want to learn more, or want to meet others who appreciate the hidden treasures that Long Island has to offer. All of these people love this island. If you show an interest in it, they will be glad to share their knowledge with you.

K.K.

Hiking Information Hub

Hiking Long Island
  P.O. Box 36
  Mount Sinai, NY 11766
  Phone: (631) 331–5938
  www.hike-li.com

Environmental Organizations

The American Littoral Society
  Northeast Chapter
  28 West 9th Road
  Broad Channel, NY 11693
  Phone: (718) 634–6467
  www.alsnyc.org

Audubon Society
  New York State Office
  200 Trillium Lane
  Albany, NY 12203
  Phone: (518) 869–9731
  www.audubon.org

Coastal Research and Education Society of Long Island, Inc.
  Southampton College of Long Island University
  Campus Box 1764
  239 Montauk Highway
  Southampton, NY 11968
  Phone: (631) 287–8223
  www.cresli.org

Cornell Cooperative Extension
  246 Griffing Avenue
  Riverhead, NY 11901-3086

Phone: (631) 727–7850
E-mail: suffolk@cce.cornell.edu

Group for the South Fork
2442 Main Street
P.O. Box 569
Bridgehampton, NY 11932
Phone: (631) 537–1400
www.thehamptons.com/group

The Long Island Group of the National Sierra Club
Phone: (516) 826–0801
www.sierraclub.org/chapters/ny/longisland/index.html

The Long Island Pine Barrens Preservation Society
P.O. Box 429
Manorville, NY 11949-9801
www.pinebarrens.org

Native America
P.O. Box 5001
Hauppauge, NY 11788
www.nativeamerica.com

The Nature Conservancy
Long Island Chapter
250 Lawrence Hill Road
Cold Spring Harbor, NY 11724
Phone: (516) 367–3225
www.tnc.org/states/newyork/longisland

The Nature Conservancy South Fork
Shelter Island Chapter
P.O. Box 5125
East Hampton, NY 11937

Phone: (631) 329–7689
www.tnc.org/states/newyork/southfork

The North Fork Environmental Council
Route 25 at Love Lane
P.O. Box 799
Mattituck, NY 11952
Phone: (631) 298–8880
www.lieast.com/nfec

The Open Space Preservation Trust, Inc.
560 South Ocean Avenue
P.O. Box 3388
Patchogue, NY 11772
Phone: (631) 474–4051

The Peconic Land Trust
P.O. Box 1776
Southampton, NY 11969
Phone: (631) 283–3195
www.peconiclandtrust.org

South Fork Natural History Society
P.O. Box Nature
Amagansett, NY 11930
Phone: (631) 267–7944
www.sofo.org

Agencies

Long Island Region–N.Y.S. Office of Parks
Recreation and Historic Preservation
Belmont Lake State Park
P.O. Box 247
Babylon, NY 11702-0247

Phone: (631) 669–1000
www.nysparks.state.ny.us

Suffolk County Parks Department
P.O. Box 144
West Sayville, NY 11796
Phone: (631) 854–4949
www.co.suffolk.ny.us/exec/parks

Hiking Groups

Appalachian Mountain Club
New York–North Jersey Chapter
5 Tudor City Place
New York, NY 10017
Voice mail: (212) 986–1430
www.amc-ny.org

Central Pine Barrens Joint Planning and Policy Commission
3525 Sunrise Highway, 2nd floor
P.O. Box 587
Great River, NY 11739-0587
Phone: (631) 224–2604
www.pb.state.ny.us

East Hampton Trails Preservation Society
P.O. Box 2144
Amagansett, NY 11930
Phone: (631) 329–4227
www.hike-li.com/ehtps/index.htm

Long Island Greenbelt Trail Conference
23 Deer Path Road
Central Islip, NY 11722-3404
Phone: (631) 360–0753
www.hike-li.com/ligtc/index.htm

Long Island Orienteering Club
  23 44th Street
  Islip, NY 11751
  Phone: (516) 567-5063
  www.everest.hunter.cuny.edu/~tbw/lioc

Nassau Hiking & Outdoor Club
  251 Lexington Avenue
  West Hempstead, NY 11552
  Phone: (516) 463-8606
  www.nhoc.org

National Wildlife Refuge (Long Island area)
  Long Island National Wildlife Refuge Complex (Wertheim NWR)
  P.O. Box 21
  Shirley, NY 11967-0021
  Phone: (631) 286-0485
  www.northeast.fws.gov/ny/lirc.htm

NY–NJ Trail Conference
  156 Ramapo Valley Road
  Mahwah, NJ 07430
  Phone: (201) 512-9348
  www.nynjtc.org

NYS Department of Environmental Conservation
  SUNY–Building 40
  Stony Brook, NY 11790
  Phone: (631) 444-0354
  www.dec.state.ny.us

Southampton Trails Preservation Society
  P.O. Box 1171
  Bridgehampton, NY 11932
  Phone: (631) 537-5202
  www.hike-li.com/stps/index.htm

Introduction

Walking is a pastime that can be carried out almost anywhere in city or country. Such a broad view of it, however, guarantees only to exercise your muscles. A nature walk, on the other hand, implies to us an event where exercise is secondary and the true goal is to relax and enjoy seeing and exploring new surroundings, to see more of the nonurban world and its flora and fauna. That's what we are hoping to bring you even on this busy island so close to New York City. We find that there are still many places where nature has held her own and, when humans have cooperated, has prospered. We've walked here for years and recommend it.

If you are also interested in bird-watching, you may know that Long Island is one of the best places on the East Coast for that activity, principally for migratory birds. It is strategically located on a major flyway, and it has a wide variety of habitats that appeal to diverse species. A number of the walks in this book are associated with particular types of birds, and there are comments on those pairings. Although there are wide seasonal variations in the visiting populations, the best time for seeing them is in spring. That's when the birds are in their best plumage for breeding, and foliage has not yet reached full summer density.

Walking on Long Island deserves a few explanatory words, since it may be different from what you expect. It takes you into bracing air, clears your mind, and sharpens your senses. It's refreshing. You don't have to scramble up many hillsides or explore dangerous terrain. There is little need for trail blazes, and the only equipment needed is comfortable clothing and reasonably stout shoes. Of course, the birder mustn't fail to bring her binoculars nor the photographer his camera, for there are abundant opportunities to use that kind of equipment.

Most of the places described in the pages that follow are best explored by two or three people, not groups. Also, it is usually the cars that are a problem ("where can we park legally?"). As a result, many towns and villages, and counties, have taken steps to limit access (parking) to the most popular recreation areas to local residents. This applies most strongly to the beaches and, to a lesser degree, parks. These restrictions, however, are enforced only from May to October (at most), when a permit to park is often required. At other times of the year, access is open, and local inquiry will tell you when and where you can park. So be attentive, quiet, and courteous—and don't litter. You'll be welcome almost everywhere.

When you organize your walks, recognize that you may sometimes need to alter your plans because a particular area has become inaccessible or off limits due to storm damage. This is most likely to apply to walks on or near the beaches, but occasionally woodland trails get blocked, too. Fortunately there are many alternative walks to be found almost everywhere on the island. Call your local hiking groups to find out which trails have recently been maintained.

Long pants and a hat will protect you from many hazards on the trail. Torn clothes are much preferable to torn skin. Be conscious of the fact that a hat will protect your hair from insects and your eyes from sweat and sun, but it will also block your upper field of vision. Look ahead and anticipate low-slung branches. If your clothes come in contact with any part of poison ivy, oak, or sumac, launder them. If your skin comes in contact with these plants' poisonous sap, wash thoroughly as soon as possible. Check with your local sporting goods store or pharmacy for special cleansing products. Most important of all, know what these plants look like.

A different situation arises with deer ticks. These tiny, pin-head-size devils have become common in fields and woodland areas. Just brushing against vegetation allows the tick to join your walk and start moving along your clothing to find a warm, soft patch of skin where it can burrow.

Walk on trails that have recently been maintained and always try to stay in the center of the path. Check well, especially around knee level, after brushing against grass or brush. After a hike, examine your body for ticks. If you find one attached to your skin, promptly use a fine-tipped tweezer to remove it. Grab the tick as close to the skin as possible and firmly tug. After removing a tick, watch to see if a rash develops. If so, contact your doctor promptly.

Not all deer ticks are infected with Lyme disease; you can be bitten several times without having a problem. However, an untreated bite may have serious medical consequences if ignored. So wear a hat, a light-colored, long-sleeved shirt, long pants, and long socks. Stretch the tops of the socks over the trouser legs to keep the ticks out, and use insect repellent.

This book is intended to give you seasonal walking choices. Perhaps in the height of summer you'll want to seek out the wooded, cooler places and walk the beaches when the swimmers have gone home. The towns also will be more appealing when the summer crowds have thinned.

But the fact is, taking a walk is almost always a good thing to do. If it's drizzling and overcast, it's a good day to walk; if it's cold or windy—or cold *and* windy—it's a good day to walk. Just dress appropriately. As Henry David Thoreau wrote, "When we walk, we naturally go to the fields and woods: what would become of us, if we walked only in a garden or a mall?"

The Atlantic Beaches

Long Island's best-known seashore is essentially a continuous, straight, 130-mile-long barrier beach of fine sand brought down over millennia as outwash from the two glacial moraines, Harbor Hill and Ronkonkoma, that form the forked backbone of the island. The beach sports some famous sections (Coney Island, Jones Beach, Fire Island, Montauk), some densely populated areas, and some miles of true seashore wilderness, but it's mostly distinguished by the different features along it, some man-made, some natural.

The ten sections of beach we've chosen to highlight draw their character more from the people who use them in summer and from the nature of the communities behind the beach than from any physical differences. Every yard of the beach is the same, every yard is different; all of it is worth visiting, exploring, and remembering in all seasons of the year. Remember especially to visit in spring and fall when bird migrations peak.

This brings up a necessary discussion about parking at the beaches. There are very few where parking is free year-round. State and county beaches usually have a charge for everyone from Memorial Day to Labor Day, with no restrictions the rest of the year. On the other hand, town and village beaches will usually have designated parking areas with signs saying PARKING BY PERMIT ONLY. These permits are normally available only to local residents, free or for a nominal charge. Nonresidents may be able to purchase one for a stiffer price.

The good news is that these permit restrictions are usually enforced only in summer (perhaps May through October or June to September), so check locally for the exact dates. Out of season, anyone is welcome to use the beaches. You will also see, however, that most beach approach roads are liberally marked with NO PARKING signs. These are enforced all year, so be sure you end up in a "permit" lot. We have tried to identify them on the maps with the symbol ⓟ.

Permits or parking fees are required for most beach parking throughout the Hamptons region during summer months. These permits can fall under the jurisdiction of either a village or township; prices vary depending on the municipality involved. Check with the local village or town hall for specific fees or permits required. For East Hampton town permit information, call (631) 324–4142; the Village Hall is at (631) 324–4150.

Beach walks are rather hard to calibrate in terms of time and effort, though we have listed mileages in many cases. Hard sand exposed by the tide makes for fairly easy walking; soft sand above the tide line or on a sand road behind the beach can be very tiring. Since all these beach walks call for you to retrace your steps to get back to the car, it may be best to time your walks so you can use the hard sand both ways.

One other caution is in order. Remember that the dunes in back of the beach are the only barrier that prevents the ocean from washing over the top in a storm and destroying whatever is behind it. This has happened countless times in the past, and so all along the coast people are asked to keep off the dunes, except at formal crossings. This prevents harm to the beach grass that helps hold the dunes in place against erosion.

We've described these beach walks in order from west to east, like all the other parts of this book, simply to be orderly; enjoy them in any sequence!

Robert Moses State Park

Fire Island stretches 32 miles from Democrat Point on the west to Moriches Inlet on the east. This barrier island features one of the world's great beaches and has, besides seventeen small summer communities, one state park (Robert Moses), one county park (Smith Point; see Walk 3), and a number of areas that form the bulk of the Fire Island National Seashore. U.S. Park Service visitor centers at Sailors Haven (see Walk 2), Watch Hill, and Smith Point provide good opportunities to learn more about this delightful area, and the main office in Patchogue is the place to turn for information (631–289–4810).

Robert Moses State Park is the westernmost 875 acres of Fire Island and is reachable by car on either the Meadowbrook or Wantagh Parkways, across the causeway and bridge that take you over Great South Bay and Fire Island Inlet to several parking fields accommodating more than 5,000 cars. It is parkway all 49 miles from New York City.

Since this broad, flat beach is walkable any time of year, you will never be alone hiking. It is something of an adventure, because its ready accessibility draws a wide assortment of people attracted by the sea, the sand, and the spaciousness of its open sky. But it is refreshing. Breathing air tempered by the sea, observing others reveling in the out-of-doors, and watching sandpipers scurry to the surf's edge then wheel away into the air as

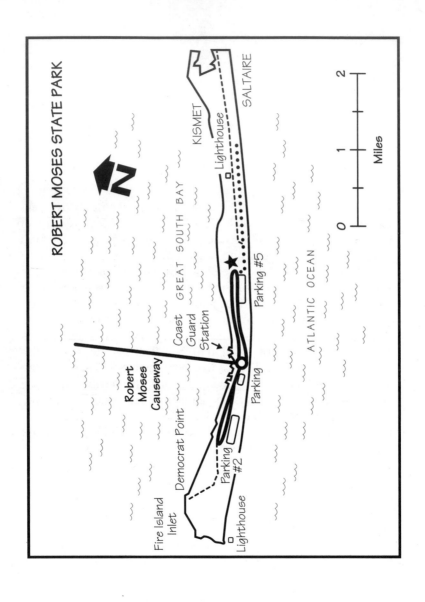

you approach will make time pass more quickly than you'd imagine. So look at your watch as you leave the parking area. There is uninterrupted beach ahead for more miles than you can walk today.

From the easternmost large parking lot (labeled FIELD 5) the distances are:

East to the lighthouse 1.4 miles
East to Kismet (first Fire Island community) 2.1 miles
East to the Sunken Forest 6.7 miles
West to Democrat Point at Fire Island Inlet 3.4 miles

The beach, known for many years as Great South Beach, is indeed great, one of the finest beaches in the world. As you visit at different seasons, you will see that it changes size and shape; it's cut away in winter, flattens out in summer. Erosion brings change, as does the longshore transport of sand by currents. The lighthouse, which was built in 1858, replaced the first one built at the western tip of the island in 1826, but the inlet is now 5 miles west of the light. The Corps of Engineers keeps dredging out the ship channel that separates it from the next island to the west, so Fire Island no longer actively grows westward.

For a short walk, head out eastward. We clock ourselves, going for about an hour, then turning around and coming back, and advise you to do the same. You will probably get to the 166-foot-tall brick lighthouse or a bit beyond.

If you do walk to the lighthouse, you will find a small museum (nominal fee) and can take a guided tour of the structure (by reservation—631–661–4876).

In September and October you are also likely to see migrating hawks seeking food to power the next leg of their shoreline migration south. Local birders will be there, too, identifying and counting the travelers, and doing their observing mostly in the stretch between the paved road and the lighthouse.

Perhaps it is best, if you seek solitude, to walk here after a storm or during the rain, when most people will not venture out.

But people flock together, and groups thin out as you go east-ward.

There are refreshment stands, picnic shelters, a first-aid station, a specially equipped playground (field 5), and a bathhouse open in season. The park is open all year, dawn to dusk. There is night fishing through December by permit. The entrance fee is $7.00 per car daily between Memorial Day and Labor Day. During autumn there is a $5.00 entry fee on weekends. There is no entry fee during winter. Fields 2 and 5 are open year-round.

2

Sailors Haven
and Sunken Forest

The waves of the great Atlantic Ocean, set in motion 600 or more miles offshore by the wind, head westward unimpeded, slide up over the continental shelf, and, with almost hourly changes of mood, strike the Long Island South Shore beaches with pulsations of fascinating and hypnotic qualities. Their visual aspects change, too, so frequently in fact that there is never a dull day at the beach. There is never the threat of oppressive crowds. It is glorious. There is a fascination that nothing can quite describe, drawing you back again and again, refreshing you—and quietly luring you into spending an hour or a day longer than you had in mind.

We have come in early spring, starting off in weather so thick we could not see Fire Island from the Sayville side, only to later see the sun break through and show off the carpet of beach heather climbing these dunes, golden in bloom.

As the barrier beach built up, collecting more and more sand, the wind piled it up and formed these dunes. While some are only 4 or 5 feet high, many, as these here, reach a height of 35 or 40 feet.

Behind the dunes, between Cherry Grove and Point O' Woods, is a sanctuary well worth a visit that affords a pleasant, wheelchair-accessible boardwalk trail. The Sunken Forest is comprised of almost forty acres of land. It is a short walk, close to Sailors Haven ferry dock. During summer the visitor center is open from 9:30 A.M. to 5:00 P.M. You will find a concessions stand,

gift shop, and rest rooms by the dock. As you cross to the south and climb the ramps protecting the dunes, you rise 35 feet above sea level and look across the top of the dunes to Great South Bay beyond.

The dense vegetation between you and the bay is the top of the forest. Now rare, although there have been many similar forests in New Jersey as well as Cape Cod, the Sunken Forest of Fire Island has fortunately been preserved, and we are able to see here many trees that are estimated to be at least a hundred years old. The principal trees are American holly, shadblow, and sassafras, grown to a height of 35 to 40 feet. Normally these species do not reach this size, because they are crowded out by stronger, taller-growing trees. Here, however, the red maple, red cedar, black and post oak, and pitch pine are themselves sheared off by the salty winds from the ocean; thus all are stunted to the protecting screen height of the dunes. The understory here was at one time a dense thicket of catbrier, Virginia creeper, and poison ivy that was alive with birds and small animals. However, the uncontrolled deer population has devastated the area by browsing on anything green, leaving only tree trunks and bare earth. As a result, almost all other animals, birds, and plants have vanished, and normal succession of trees seems very unlikely.

The boardwalk comes out on the bayside into almost blinding light if it is a bright day, through thickets of phragmites reeds, hugs the sandy shore, and reenters the forest to the west, twining back through the area. On a hot summer day, it's pleasantly cool.

To reach Sailors Haven, take the ferry (passengers only—no cars) from River Road, Sayville. Be prepared to pay a fee for parking by the ferry dock. From May through November, the ferry usually operates on a regular schedule. After the summer season, service ends to Sailors Haven but continues all winter, on a limited basis, from Sayville to Cherry Grove and Fire Island Pines, which are 1 or 2 miles away on foot. Another option is to take the Ocean Beach ferry from Bay Shore—with a 3-mile walk. Call the ferries for schedules: (631) 589–8980 in Sayville, (631) 665–3600 in Bay Shore; or try the Sailors Haven ranger station at (631) 597–6210 for more information.

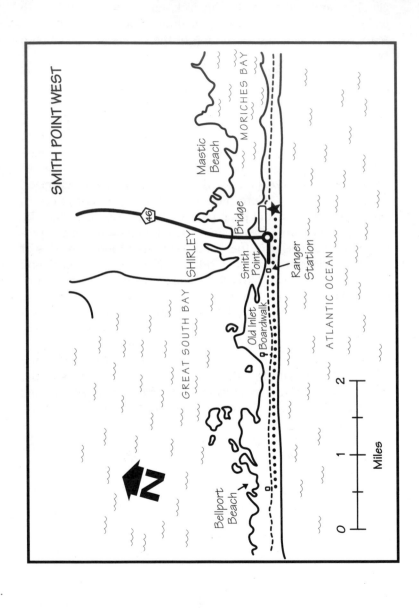

3

Smith Point

The beach accessible at Smith Point is one of our favorite places to walk. The 7-mile stretch westward to Watch Hill is presently the only federal wilderness area in New York State and consequently is not open to vehicles (although specially permitted four-wheel-drive vehicles may drive on the ocean beach only). A causeway and bridge lead to the eastern end of the island, where there's ample parking. (The summer parking fee is $8.00 for non–Suffolk County residents and $5.00 for residents with a green key card.) This is at the south end of the William Floyd Parkway. Train service on the Montauk line goes to Shirley Station, 2.5 miles from the bridge. The facilities at this county park include camping, picnic areas, fishing, and a disabled-accessible playground. For information call (631) 852-1313.

A two-story, octagonal visitor center on the dunes houses the national seashore ranger's office (631–281–3010), which is open year-round and contains an informative display on beach life. If you call, be sure to ask if a summer nature walk is available.

The beach westward offers a walk stretchable as far as you'll be able to go. We usually head for the Old Inlet, which is about a 2-mile round trip. The national seashore maintains a shower–rest room building there during summer and an ocean-to-bay board-walk as well as a small dock with a buoy-marked channel leading to it. In moderate or cold weather, it's nice to come back on the sand trail (formerly used as a road) that runs inland parallel to the ocean.

At low tide a colorful array of pebbles is exposed that may get you started on a pebble collection! White, black, red, brown, lavender, and those with subtle variations are available in a seemingly limitless supply. In fact, that's where all the sand comes from—the rocks and stones beat against each other, reducing themselves into smaller and smaller pieces. Scoop up these dry sands and, as they run through your fingers, investigate them carefully. At least half the sand is quartz, but you'll also find hornblende, rutile, feldspar, augite, magnetite, ilmenite—a variety of names to confound you or just possibly to start you exploring a whole new world of minerals and rocks. Below Hatteras, down into the beaches of the South, much of the sand is made up of tiny shell fragments, but not here on Long Island. Shells are relatively scarce. The rocks that make up these beaches were brought by the mighty glaciers of the Ice Age all the way from Canada. So as you inspect the debris of the sand, you might find anything. They tell us specks of ruby and emerald exist here—but rarely! However, if you search, you'll certainly find garnet. And the black patches contain magnetite, an important iron ore that sometimes becomes magnetized; when it does, it's called lodestone. If you run a magnet through this, you'll find that particles will cling.

With no people living on this thin stretch of the barrier beach, a walk here exposes some of the fragile links in the chain of life. For among the variety of life zones—the tidal edge of the sea, the beach itself, behind the sandy swales of the dunes, and in the wetlands along the Great South Bay—is a busy world to capture your interest and excite your imagination. We see hoofprints of deer here often, but deer are remarkable in becoming invisible. Only once or twice have we actually seen them here.

Quogue and Tiana Beaches

Cross the bridge at Quogue or Hampton Bays onto Dune Road. About midway between the two is Tiana Beach, where there's parking and easy access across the dunes.

Wide and open, the beach here is strung out with cottages just behind the dunes, but they don't dominate the landscape. We generally walk a mile west, by the round apartment complex and several summer places to Quogue Public Beach, and return. Then we walk another mile east to total an hour and a half or two hours of elapsed time. It is never too crowded.

Low tide is the best time to walk on the beach, because the wet sand is compact and settled by the waves. So all along the water's edge, the firm walkway is hard enough not to hold you back in your own footsteps. Actually, water still remains between the individual grains of sand; even on the hottest days, the sun dries only the surface. There's a microscopic world of channels and ponds teeming with almost invisible life. Just watch the tiny sandpipers scurrying up to the water's edge, pecking away at the oozing sand. That's what they're after.

Quite apart from our walks, however, something else compels us to come back here. That is Dune Road. The variety of shorebirds using the wetlands along the north of the road is almost endless. Nearly all the creatures that nest or visit Long Island can be seen at some spot along here, wading in the shallows,

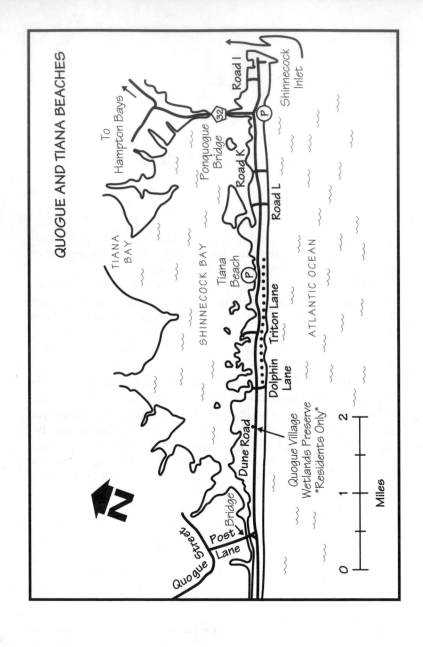

QUOGUE AND TIANA BEACHES

To Hampton Bays

TIANA BAY

SHINNECOCK BAY

Ponquogue Bridge

32

Road I

Shinnecock Inlet

Road K

Road L

P

Tiana Beach

ATLANTIC OCEAN

P

Triton Lane

Dolphin Lane

Quogue Village Wetlands Preserve *Residents Only*

Dune Road

Post Lane

Bridge

Quogue Street

N

0   1   2

Miles

standing in the grass, or winging low over the water. During the migratory season you will see one or two dunlins, black-bellied plovers, ruddy turnstones, and then another and another, until you realize that the grass or shoreline is alive with them.

Come equipped with glasses and your bird guide. You'll find your car a perfect blind from which to observe. Drive along slowly. We've seen and heard the clapper rail, with his raucous call, and watched the bittern slowly swaying as he holds his bill in the air pretending to be a reed, trying to elude us. And we have watched black skimmer after black skimmer feeding, with their precision glide along the water. You'll see it all on Dune Road. Travel to the ends of the roads that intersect Dune Road between Post Lane and Shinnecock Inlet. There are excellent views of marshes, sandbars, jetties, and bay to the north and dunes and seashore to the south.

The slimy wetlands swarm with insects, and the water is unfit to drink. But acre for acre, the salt marsh will produce more plants than any farm, fertilizing itself, needing no help from humans in planting or harvesting. Not only is it the feeding ground for the migrating birds you see along Dune Road, but it provides shelter and food for small mammals as well. We've watched the muskrat swimming here and working in the shallows, for example. And the tiny fish that swim and breed here are carried out on tides to feed larger fish miles from shore.

5

Southampton Beach

From Shinnecock Inlet in Southampton eastward, the beach stretches in a broad unbroken swath for 11 miles to Sagaponack Pond. In summer this area attracts, for the most part, those who are content to lie out in the sun, dip in the magnificent surf—sometimes it's too magnificent and must be respected—and picnic or fling the Frisbee. Off season it is almost completely uninhabited except for the occasional dog walker, surf angler, or bird-watcher.

There are many public access areas where you may park. Sometimes there is a fee, or a parking permit is required (obtained at the Southampton Village or one of the town halls or at the beach). Out of season, however, there should be no problem.

This stretch is characterized by high dunes; rather large summerhouses, usually set well behind the dunes for protection; a number of guarded beaches for swimming; good walking at low tide; and many ponds just behind the dunes, where there is always more to see than a bird. At the east end of Shinnecock Bay, the beach ceases to be a barrier island (or here a peninsula) and all the rest of the way to Montauk becomes part of the mainland. These are classic beaches, the kind you see in marvelous color prints—the dunes covered with pale chartreuse grasses, the sun catching the movement of the waves, and a mist of salt spray hanging over the broad stretches of white sand.

At the Shinnecock or western end of this stretch, there are no buildings at all and the dunes are unusually high. Terns must nest here, for once in spring they literally dive-bombed us. Parking out here is informal. The road peters out, so be careful unless you have a four-wheel-drive vehicle. The walk to the jetty is about 2 miles.

There are three or four other accesses to the beach. Our favorite section to walk is the one locally known as Fowlers. The approach to the high dunes is past a couple of ponds through broad potato fields, some seasons planted in wheat for rotation. Parking is in a lot off the road just before the dunes, so your walk is first to get to the beach. There are usually interesting birds on both sides of the ponds, and in August they are surrounded by the huge pink or rose flowers of the marsh mallow. We turn left as we come onto the beach, walk along the water to Mecox Bay and back, making a total distance of just over 3 miles. To visit the shore east of Mecox Bay, follow Mecox Road south to the end of Jobs Lane, where you will find a town parking area. If you continue about 0.5 mile to Dune Road, you will see a Nature Conservancy sign, MECOX DUNES, on your left. This preserve is open to the public. Here you can observe shorebirds on Mecox Bay and the surrounding salt marsh.

Beach walks clear your mind of many things. Often personal problems are replaced by other thoughts worth consideration, like the fact that geologists say these beaches are a million years old!

For a change of scene while in Southampton, it might be interesting to visit the Dupont Nature Sanctuary, at the southeast end of Captains Neck Lane. It harbors a true salt-marsh ecosystem that forms a kind of natural barrier between ocean and land. It provides a resilient buffer against the forces of storm and tide, but, most important, it represents the first link in the food chain. This is where organic matter decays to feed ever-larger organisms, from plankton to fish to people.

6

Wainscott Beach

Of the five unbroken stretches of beach along Long Island's south shore, Wainscott Beach, 3.6 miles from end to end, is the shortest. Many walkers have a compulsion to cover every mile of a stretch, just because it is there, and it's easy to understand the urge because it is satisfying to traverse any stretch. Still, on the broad, flat strands of the coastline here, there aren't any startling discoveries. One beach is very much like another. There are differences, of course, but these differences are subtle, sometimes more metaphysical than real. And since, from hour to hour, aspects of the beach-walking experience change anyway, it can be misleading to describe any of Long Island's beaches in specific detail. Wainscott Beach is probably the most out of the way. There are cottages all along, well back in grassy stretches, and the dunes are lower. For some reason driftwood does not accumulate here to the extent it does farther east. Freighters at sea seem farther out.

To reach Wainscott Beach, turn south from the Montauk Highway 1.3 miles east of Bridgehampton on Sagg Main Street to Sagaponack, and on to the end; or go to the end of Beach Lane in Wainscott.

It's a good idea to check the tide tables before you start off and try to do your principal walking during low tide, when the footing is more solid and the walking easier! Up on the higher

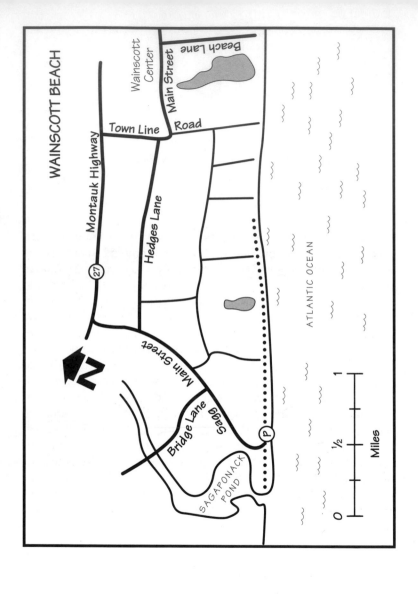

WAINSCOTT BEACH

ground, the surface sand does dry to a greater depth, and walking becomes more laborious.

When you stand on the beach facing the sea, you can notice from many little indicators that the water pulls to the west. For the longest time we simply couldn't understand this. We'd say that the Gulf Stream was out there moving eastward and northward along the coast, so how could the water here along shore move as it obviously does, in the opposite direction? Have you asked yourself this question? Have you seen how the sand moves west with the currents, how pieces of driftwood move back toward New York? In a word, the answer is friction. The Gulf Stream is a very large river, about 40 miles wide and 2,000 feet deep, with a volume of water a thousand times larger than our biggest river, and it moves about 5.5 miles per hour in a northeasterly direction. As it moves, the water along the shore is set into countercurrents and eddies that flow for a time in the reverse direction because of the friction of the shore.

7

East Hampton Beach

From Georgica Pond, Long Island South Beach is uninterrupted for 22.2 miles to Montauk. Locally the stretch is referred to as East Hampton Beach, Amagansett Beach, Napeague Beach, or Montauk Beach, depending on its proximity to the adjoining community. The entire stretch is magnificent and eminently walkable.

Parking on East Hampton beaches is restricted to residents only during the season. The town of East Hampton is chic, beautifully maintained, and handsome, with tree-shaded lanes and many attractive houses. It has a casual dignity and considerable local civic pride. We've driven along streets here early in the morning, before breakfast, on the way to the beach and seen golden pheasants, one after another, strutting across village greenswards. This pastoral, relaxed village atmosphere is the secret of East Hampton's jealously guarded charm, and a strong effort is being made to keep it this way.

A good walk on East Hampton Beach is from the village beach east of Hook Pond; walk westward to the Georgica Pond inlet and return. The total distance, round trip, is 6.4 miles. On your right as you head out will be the Maidstone Golf Club and Hook Pond, which is a good birding area. Beyond Main Street Beach the dune area is fairly primitive, low and windswept. Off season you can find a place to park.

The beach here is in striking contrast to, say, the beaches west of Jones Beach, where our urban sprawl has crowded out the dunes. The charm and attractiveness of eastern Long Island is threatened by growth—the statistically predictable population explosion and overcrowding that seem inevitable. East Hampton is vigorously trying to preserve its heritage, limit its growth, and save its open land for living space. As you walk Long Island, you will appreciate its openness and see the need to save its wild areas.

Amagansett Beach

An easy direct access to Amagansett Beach is to turn south off the Montauk Highway onto the Indian Wells Highway (2.5 miles east of East Hampton, but before you reach Amagansett). At its end is a bathhouse on the east side, and opposite this, Sheppard's Dunes, an eight-acre area acquired and protected by The Nature Conservancy to preserve its natural state. Parking during the season is reserved for residents. It's better to walk in late spring or early fall anyway.

The beach itself has character. Houses sit almost 0.5 mile up from the beach on bluffs overlooking the sea, and the dunes are wild. So our suggestion is to walk to Maidstone Golf Club, which is 2.5 miles to the west on the wide beach, then return.

For anyone who has lived in inland wooded areas, the plants and ground cover of the seashore offer a fascinating world of discovery. When there's a break in the dunes, as there is here, you may be tempted to cross in order to examine interior plant life. But don't do it. You will crush the dune grasses, making the passage vulnerable to wind erosion. And just one such spot can actually weaken an entire dune. So be conservation minded and alert to damage to any plant life. You will be able to find a path allowing you to observe.

The beach grass, with its long, curving leaves, is the principal stabilizer for the dunes. It gets its nourishment from windblown

minerals, grows up, sends its roots deep, and follows the contours of the dunes. The false heather is another, with bright buttery yellow blossoms on view May through July. It is a low, shrubby plant adapted to life on the shifting sands.

Just over the dunes, when there's soil enough, the beach pea will take hold, sending its vinelike leaflets swarming, the ends with little tendrils like a pig's tail. You will want to examine the pea flowers, which are delicate in shades of violet and purple, blossoming throughout the summer. Inland, thickets of beach plum and bayberry take hold with beautiful fruit in fall.

When the dunes are stabilized, the exuberance that nature displays is amazing. Above all, you should beware of poison ivy, rampant near the beach. You will find rugosa rose, seaside goldenrod, thistle, and blueberry. It is really quite startling to realize the wide variety of plant life near the beach.

NAPEAGUE BEACH

NAPEAGUE BAY

NAPEAGUE HARBOR

ATLANTIC OCEAN

Hither Woods

State Park

Old Montauk

Camping

W

Cranberry Hole Road

Paumanok Path

Montauk Highway

27

L.I.R.R.

W

N

Miles

0   ½   1

9

Napeague Beach

After you leave Amagansett, driving east, the ocean comes into view from the highway for the first time. The peninsula abruptly narrows; two bodies of water—Napeague Bay and Harbor—extend southward, making the land here less than a mile wide until you reach Hither Hills (about 6 miles). The road parallels the ocean about 0.5 mile inland. The land is flat with low dunes and familiar seaside plants. Napeague Beach extends eastward from Amagansett.

If you wish to enter Napeague State Park from its western boundary, there is a small parking area on Cranberry Hole Road. Just beyond the Long Island Rail Road tracks on the right side of the road, you'll find parking space on the shoulder. If you are adventurous, you may wish to walk the white-blazed Paumanok Path through the low-growing oak and pine maritime woods to the harbor 2.5 miles to the east.

It's easiest to get onto the beach through Hither Hills State Park, however. This is a good place to get a feeling for the forces that shaped Long Island's topographic features. As you leave Amagansett, you see the high dunes petering out; then at Hither Hills the landmass piles up again, now in contours and hills that are more than 150 feet above sea level. The landmasses are the result of the moraine pushed here by the glaciers and modified ever since by the continuous action of wind and sea. Great rolling breakers have been moving in on the Long Island shoreline for a million years since the first glacier came down, and for more than 25,000 years since the last, scooping up rocks and sand, rubbing and grinding, and depositing the very fine particles that form the present continuous beach. And the wind has blown it around. What with storms and tides and longshore transit of sands by currents, there have been constant changes in elevations and shorelines. It is recorded that there were seven inlets east of Fire Island in 1743—but then Fire Island was 55 miles long. It was not until 1931 that big waves and high tides separated the dunes and broke through Fire Island at Moriches Inlet in a destructive storm. And it is inevitable that there will be further change.

As you walk Napeague Beach, go east for a time and see the high bluffs where the Ronkonkoma Moraine comes right to the sea. Turn around and walk past the park to the low dunes. Along the way you will surely see an angler or two.

Offshore the bottom is even and shoals quite gradually, and you will generally see commercial and sport-fishing boats trolling along here, as the fishing is apt to be good. At least surfcasters have this attitude. During summer there are schools of bluefish, sea bass, porgies, and flounder. Late in autumn striped bass can be caught and, through the winter, cod.

10

Montauk Beach

There's a gap in the morainal hills that defines Montauk Beach—about a 3.5-mile stretch of broad sandy beach below the high dunes along the Old Montauk Highway. East of this you come to the 70-foot-high bluffs, a kind of land's end, halfway between New York City and the farthest reach of Cape Cod, which is Montauk Point. Kirk Park Beach, right in town, is a popular spot all year, since access is easy and the beach is nice and wide. There will be bathers and people lying in the sun if it's summer. And if you walk west toward the dunes, you should surely see surfers in wet suits, because the conditions are evidently good there.

For a less busy area with bluffs you can walk on, visit Shadmoor State Preserve. This preserve was recently purchased through the cooperative efforts of New York State, Suffolk County, East Hampton, and The Nature Conservancy. It's bordered on the north by the parkway and on the south by the ocean, so you need not be overly concerned about getting lost on this one-hundred acre preserve. During our last visit a silver fox accompanied us while we viewed a wide range of birds. The diverse habitats include woods, grasslands, shrublands, and ocean.

While walking the maze of trails, you will come upon several deteriorating cement bunkers. They were part of the communications and defense network that coordinated the large guns located at Camp Hero. This network protected us from an oceanborne attack during World War II. It becomes obvious why this was such an ideal place to build bunkers when you ap-

proach the breathtaking panoramic view from the bluffs. The gracefully fluted bluffs themselves are a natural home for the large colony of bank swallows in residence.

The park is 0.7 mile east of the Montauk village green on the south side of Route 27. A large sign at a cleared area (it will one day be a designated parking area) identifies the entrance. You may be ticketed for parking alongside the parkway, so try Fox Street, on the north side of the Montauk Highway a short distance to the west. Park on the shoulder adjacent to where the Paumanok Path parkway trail crosses over the street. You can follow this trail east until you are opposite the park entrance and then cross the road. If you are fortunate enough to be an East Hampton town resident, you may prefer to park at the Ditch Plains bathing beach, in the residents-only lot, and enter Shadmoor via the Rheinstein Park trail.

The best surfing waves are known as spilling breakers—those that, as they approach the beach, have a line of foam spilling down their front, always just about to break but holding off for quite a while. The more gradual the slope of the bottom, the longer the wave will hold off breaking; thus the best surfing is on the kind of beach that has a long stretch underwater with almost no slope at all.

There is never a day on these waters when there is no surf whatsoever, though it is possible for it to be too dull for those who make a sport of it. The whole science of waves is complex, but it is interesting to know that a wave will break when the ratio of the height of the wave to the depth of water is about three to four; that is, a 6-foot wave will break in about 8 feet of water.

The wave action is caused principally by the wind's force against the surface of the water. The water itself actually moves very little. You can see this when you watch a cork or piece of driftwood bobbing at sea; after the wave has passed, you see how little the cork has moved. When a wave passes through very shallow waters, it lifts and stirs up sand from the bottom, so the loose grains of sand settle in a different place than where they started. That's how waves change and shape the contours of beaches.

Towns to Explore on Foot

One of the joys of walking is to step out of the fetters of time, to while away and unwind at a leisurely pace and with a certain detachment. Keeping alert to the surroundings in this carefree state, you'll experience a feeling of satisfaction. Walking along the edge of the sea may give you a sense of leaping back in time, and walking along narrow streets of an old village may make you feel nostalgic, feeding your hankering for a simpler life.

Long Island was colonized by New Englanders, mostly from Connecticut, and English architectural influences are visible in a number of places, some dating as far back as the Old House in Cutchogue (1649). There are Dutch influences, too, which pushed eastward from New Amsterdam.

Rural village charms that still exist on Long Island are mainly left over from the nineteenth century. By then the settlements had established a character that has strong appeal to us today. There are other communities you might want to explore besides the six we describe here. They offer interesting architecture and retain vestiges of rural village charms. We suggest you investigate *Amityville,* south of Farmingdale at the end of Broad Hollow Road and south of the Sunrise Highway; *Roslyn Park,* just south of the North Hempstead Turnpike between Port Washington Boulevard and Glen Cove Road; and the hamlet of *Oyster Bay,* all in Nassau County. And in Suffolk County visit *Cold Spring Harbor,* on the North Hempstead Turnpike, 2 miles west of Huntington; and *Northport,* east of Huntington and Centerport, north of Route 25A. There's an old pre-Revolutionary church on Main Street at the Setauket Green in *Setauket,* west and north of Port Jefferson.

Riverhead is also a town worth visiting, but not for New England charm, which is largely absent. The real reason to visit is the small but excellent Suffolk County Historical Society Museum at 300 West Main Street. It houses a unique collection of artifacts reflecting more than three centuries of change. Household objects and furniture, Native American items, farm and maritime tools, and buggies and carts provide an honest glimpse of Long Island's history. It is worth noting that Riverhead is very convenient for accessing nearly half the walks we have listed. The museum is open Tuesday, Wednesday, Thursday, and Saturday from 12:30 to 4:30 P.M., but phone before going to be sure (631–727–2881). Admission is free, donations are welcome, and the gift shop has an unparalleled variety of books about Long Island.

Douglas Manor

Douglas Manor is a community of cozy-looking houses set on a peninsula that juts into Little Neck Bay at the eastern end of Queens County. It is that part of Douglaston that lies entirely north of the tracks of the Port Washington Branch of the Long Island Rail Road, and we think you would really enjoy the walk around the peninsula, along a sidewalk by the water's edge much of the way. If you come by train, get off at the Douglaston station. By car, leave Northern Boulevard on the Douglaston Parkway and head north past the station area until you find a place to park. That may mean looking for several blocks, especially during the week, when commuters are here in numbers.

Start your walk on the west side by going down 36th Avenue to the shore road and then heading north along Little Neck Bay. In summer this is a very popular place for shorebirds and modest sailboats. The waters are unusually clean, largely due to the total absence of commercial activities and marinas. Once you round the north point and head down Marinette Street and Douglas Road, you'll be on the edge of a small park and a large, marshy wildlife preserve that extends over to the far shore. To return to your starting point from the end of Douglas Road, just turn right onto Hillside Avenue and continue over the hill to West Drive. The total walking distance, starting at the station, is about 2.5 mostly level miles.

If you take the additional time to explore the streets of Douglas Manor, which we recommend, you will quickly sense that it is an unusual community. Although there are a few old houses, one dating to 1732, the town's history dates to around 1906, when the Douglas Estate was developed into a railroad or "garden" suburb and planned according to a radical notion at the time: cooperative ownership of the mile-long waterfront. The 590 houses represent every architectural style of the early twentieth century, including Queen Anne, Colonial, Tudor, and Mediterranean Revival, and range from virtual cottages to mansions. Many enjoy fine water views.

Recognition as a special place has also come through its designation by the city as one of New York's historic districts.

There has always been a strong bent here for community improvement, as evidenced by the fact that it has the largest community garden club in New York State. In another sense Douglas Manor is nearly an arboretum, because well over one hundred varieties of trees have been introduced over the years. The streets are graced by innumerable giants, topped by a 600-year-old white oak at 233 Arleigh Road. Many rare and exotic varieties are also to be found.

All in all there is much to catch your eye here—not only the water traffic you would expect on the sound and in the bay, but also the wildlife, which is abundant for so densely populated a county.

12

Sea Cliff

"The style of the houses in Sea Cliff," says one local resident with a measure of civic pride, "is what we call 'Carpenter Gothic.'" Perhaps this sets in your mind's eye a village that is a collection of highly individual gingerbread houses that have been lovingly attended to over the years. Actually there's an ample supply of larger, well-maintained Victorian ones as well, not to mention a real diversity in more modern varieties. You should enjoy a walk in Sea Cliff for surprises! It rolls comfortably over high bluffs overlooking Hempstead Harbor. Narrow streets running up and down steep slopes, some very small parcels of land, and loving care are the complementary parts that make up a whole picture of Sea Cliff that forms as you trudge around the town on foot.

Start off by parking near Clifton Park and walk westward along Sea Cliff Avenue. There are some big houses here, and you'll cross through the business district, perhaps quickly sensing that the principal industry these days is selling antiques. When you reach Central Avenue, detour briefly around to the north side of the Village Hall (former Methodist church) to visit the Sea Cliff Museum. It is the community's response to the unique historical background of the town and has interesting artifacts and photographs from the past. An interesting booklet called *This Is Sea Cliff* describes the background of the village, the many parks, and other points of interest. It costs $2.00, and it can also be bought in the Village Hall during normal business hours (516–671–0080). Hours for the museum are Saturday and Sunday from 2:00 to 5:00 P.M. (January and February from 2:00 to 4:00 P.M.); closed in summer. For more information call (516) 671–0090.

Return to Sea Cliff Avenue and continue west. Shortly you will reach Memorial Park, site of an old inn, which was seized and demolished by the town for back taxes. The property is on the heights, and you will come upon a grand view of Long Island Sound.

Walk north on Prospect Avenue, left down Cliffway, and north again on The Boulevard. Two sets of steps will bring you back up to Prospect. A longer alternate walk is to go from Memorial Park south down Prospect Avenue to the shoreline and follow it as it curves along under the lovely old plane trees (sycamores) to Scudders Pond. Returning, you can explore the narrow streets along Sea Cliff's "Cliff Side" by following Littleworth Lane back up to Carpenter, thence along it to Glen Avenue and the park.

The first gathering of people here was really a Methodist summer camp meeting with tents, picnics, and summer smiles on the faces of earnest cityfolk, singing hymns on the wooded hills above the water, away from the ruffians of the city. That was in 1865. Good steamboat service to New York City was available and convenient from the pier in the harbor. The church group later bought 240 acres from the Carpenter family, who owned the farmlands, and divided it. The atmosphere was so congenial that people eventually built little houses on their 40-by-60-foot lots to make the camp more permanent and lavished every spare dollar they could to make it attractive.

By 1895, however, word of its charms having spread, Sea Cliff had become a very popular summer resort, and many large Victorian houses had been built. There was a cable car up the cliff, and a boardwalk had been built along the shorefront. The Long Island Rail Road was running trains into the little gingerbread station on a regular schedule, spring, summer, and fall, and there were four boats daily between Sea Cliff and New York. Today it stands as one of the best-preserved little square miles around.

13

Old Bethpage Village Restoration

Unlike the other communities, Old Bethpage Village is a restoration, a composite made up of simple houses and shops with some architectural merit, regrouped here on a 200-acre site ample enough to provide a proper setting for the buildings and re-create the atmosphere of a mid-nineteenth-century village. And it is a pleasant surprise. We think it makes a delightful walk, a lovely switch in centuries.

You will find a parking lot and a reception center of contemporary design, as well as an adequate cafeteria, an excellent gift shop, and a small auditorium showing a film on the restoration. A $6.00 admission fee is charged, with reductions for senior citizens and children. Allow a couple of hours and spend another if you can make the time.

We walked into the days before the mechanization of the farm. This illusion is skillfully achieved. The dirt path we followed is bordered by a post-and-rail fence; the field through which it ambled lay fallow, but liberally sprinkled with Queen Anne's lace and butterflies. Birds chirped. There was the faint, not unpleasant, organic smell that emanates from a farmyard.

We were greeted at one of the houses by an eager youth who showed us through what had once been a bayman's dwelling.

OLD BETHPAGE
VILLAGE
RESTORATION

N

Parking ★

Visitor
Center

Fairgrounds

Store

Church

Inn

School

Black-
smith

Powell
Farm

POND

Miles

0   1/10   2/10

Uncluttered, simply furnished, it set an informal, friendly tone for our visit. Altogether forty-five buildings, all original structures, have been saved from destruction and moved here to form a charming nineteenth-century village.

At the crossroads is a general store, with the proprietor's living quarters under the same roof, an inn serving root beer in the Tap Room, and a blacksmith's forge. By this time we had noticed that all the guides were dressed in clothes of the period. It is not correct to say that they were wearing costumes—the garb is simple, functional, and doesn't at first catch your eye.

The Powell farm is functioning. There are pigs and cows, chickens and geese. The ladies were baking bread, and a pot of soup hung simmering from the crane over coals smoldering away in the fireplace. It was vegetable soup, and the gardens had provided all the ingredients. The flies buzzed, a Canada goose honked, and the old sow lay sprawled out in the mud.

It is an uncluttered, friendly, helpful little valley, and the attitudes of all the people working here make it so.

The walk around the loop is 1.5 miles. During the school year we were told there are daily groups—so our suggestion is to come, as we did, on a summer's day. Let the natural breezes provide the stream to float your daydreams on. Lengthen your stride, but slow down your pace, and reflect how downright simple the necessities of life can be. The 1.5-mile walk plus the other exploring footsteps will add up to enough on a hot afternoon.

Remember, though, that the village is open and alive all year (except January and February), with daily hours from 10:00 A.M. to 5:00 P.M.; so it is possible to experience a variety of activities having to do with the passing of the seasons. For specific schedules and information, call (516) 572–8400.

The entrance to the village is on the east side of Round Swamp Road, about 1 mile south of the Long Island Expressway (Route 495), exit 48.

STONY BROOK

WEST MEADOW CREEK

SMITHTOWN BAY

West Meadow

Christian Avenue

MUSEUMS

A

C

H

25A

North Country Road

PORPOISE CHANNEL

Village

Main Street

Grist Mill

Mill Pond

Museums

25A

0   ¼   ½

Miles

Stony Brook

Because Stony Brook village is old and handsome, we think you should see it for its unique charm and Long Island bayside country atmosphere.

Visitors will be interested in the complex of buildings now known as the Long Island Museum of Art, History and Carriages (formerly the Museums at Stony Brook). Founded in the 1930s, the museums comprise the largest privately supported museum complex in the region. They include three major exhibition buildings and a number of eighteenth- and nineteenth-century historic structures. Their overall theme is the exhibition and interpretation of American art and history. Thus in the Margaret Melville Blackwell History Museum (H), you'll find special exhibitions on historical themes, a gallery of period rooms (in miniature), and a superb collection of antique decoys. The Art Museum (A) also features changing shows, along with permanent displays of works by William Sidney Mount (1807–68), the celebrated Long Island genre painter.

The original heart of the complex is now known as the Ward and Dorothy Melville Carriage House (C). It displays more than one hundred vehicles illustrating the history of horse-drawn transportation. The carts, cabs, coaches, broughams, phaetons, wagons, sleighs, and fire engines are all a delight to see. A Pleasure Driving section is but one of nine that help make this one of the finest such collections in the country.

When you visit Stony Brook (take Route 25A north from Smithtown), you can park either at the museums or on the waterfront. If you choose the former, go first to the History Museum (H) for admission tickets ($4.00 for adults). After seeing the three main buildings, you can also visit the blacksmith shop and schoolhouse. Be sure to leave enough time to walk north along Main Street about 0.5 mile into the village, passing the Mill Pond with its resident families of waterfowl and water lilies, and stopping at the interesting old gristmill, which is in full operation. It is open April through December; phone the Ward Melville Heritage Organization, formerly known as the Community Fund, which owns it, at (631) 751–2244 for exact days and hours.

As you come to the village green, you'll find a variety of interesting shops on your right, and the waterfront ahead on your left. The bay and salt meadows here supply New England scene as you might imagine. It is not difficult to see how the English settlers who came here from Suffolk chose these shores or why it reminded them of their native country. It's also easy to understand the overwhelmingly important part played by the sea, bays, and water routes in the first 200 years of Long Island's development.

Heading toward the town parking lot and waterfront, you will pass the *Discovery* dock and a marina where motorboat and canoe rentals are available. Continue north along West Meadow Creek for a lovely short walk. If you can, take time to enjoy a one-and-a-half-hour trip around the harbor and wetlands for an interpretive tour embracing ecology, geology, and history on the *Discovery*. Its schedule depends on the tides, so it is constantly changing. For reservations call (631) 751–2244. Bring your binoculars and camera.

Stony Brook village is clean and tidy and has an air of nostalgia. You can walk along, window-shopping and dating old houses as you return to your starting point, but surely you will have lost track of time on the way.

Although the museums are open all year, both hours and admission fees are subject to change. We suggest that you telephone in advance (631–751–0066) to get current information on hours and special exhibitions, or visit the Web site: www.stonybrookvillage.com.

15

Sag Harbor

Sag Harbor, a National Historic District, is certainly one of the best-preserved old villages on Long Island, with hedges and picket fences and curving, crooked, and shaded streets that are lined with charming houses.

Starting at the chamber of commerce windmill on the waterfront, walk along Bay Street and on to the Long Wharf, observe the coastal activity, inspect the windmill on Main Street at the waterfront, shop at any one of the numerous little stores and markets in the area, or stroll in the Marine Park or yacht club area. If you wish, look across the harbor from the North Haven Bridge to Shelter Island in the north. Then walk up Main Street as far as you like. The finest example of Greek Revival architecture in New York State, built in 1845, now houses the revitalized Whaling and Historical Museum (631–725–0770), which attracts more than 35,000 people seasonally; you walk through a whale's jaws as you enter. (It is open daily May 15 through the end of September.) Across Garden Street is the Hannibal French House, a large Victorian mansion, now painted a pleasant, dark ivory color, and the old Custom House, which is a National Landmark and the home and office of the first customs collector of New York State. Sag Harbor was named an official Port of Entry in 1789 by President George Washington, and a U.S. Post Office was initiated by Postmaster General Benjamin Franklin.

On side streets—wander off on any of them—you'll see many

SAG HARBOR

NORTH HAVEN

SAG HARBOR COVE

Light

Long Wharf

Whaling Museum

Garden

Main

Madison

Union

Bay Street

Cemetery

Division

Easthampton Road

Sagg

0   ¼   ½

Miles

fine little houses built during prosperous days, from the late eighteenth century to the mid–nineteenth. They have simple lines in the style of that era. These residential streets have been restored with care, painted, and nicely planted by their present owners, giving you an indication of the prosperity of the past.

You should turn left at the museum and go along Union Street past Madison to see the First Presbyterian Church of Sag Harbor—locally known as the Whalers Church—based on Egyptian style and something of a curiosity. The spyglass-shaped steeple that once dominated the town was blown down in the hurricane of 1938 and never replaced. All the architectural trim is said to have been hand-carved by whalers from the village. And nearby, the old graveyard is interesting. A lovelier-looking church is Christ Episcopal, farther down Madison.

First there was a little fishing village started here in 1665 by a small band of Narragansetts, traditional rivals of the Montauks and Shinnecocks. Then the white settlers moved in around 1707. Although known for a time as Sterling Bay (after the English Lord Sterling), it eventually took the name Sag Harbor, being the harbor of Sagg, a little settlement near what is now Bridgehampton, a corruption of the native name Saggabonac: "where the ground nuts [potatoes] grow"!

At the end of the eighteenth century, Sag Harbor cleared a greater tonnage of goods than New York Harbor, and it was to become one of the principal whaling ports on the Atlantic seacoast, second only to New Bedford. Between 1790 and 1870 more than 500 voyages were made from here, and the whale oil brought back to light the cities and houses of New England was valued at $25 million. There were once sixty-three vessels registered here. The population reached 3,500 by 1843. Rough seamen walked these very streets you roam today—Montauk and Shinnecock Indians, but also Fijians, Hawaiians, Malays, Ethiopians, and Portuguese.

After the Civil War the whaling industry had a rapid decline, and Sag Harbor's fortunes dwindled. Today tourism and light manufacturing are a boon.

16

Orient

Places on earth, like people, seem to develop under current conditions along conforming lines. One airport looks pretty much like any other, anywhere in our world, and cities and houses fall into similar categories. Those places that guard their character from external forces and preserve their antiquities develop an aura that is often admirable. Little villages lying somewhere along headwaters tend to preserve this aura, and the hamlet of Orient, lying the farthest east of any of the settlements on the northern fork, quite off the beaten track, has perhaps the greatest individuality of any place on Long Island.

We hope, in saying this, that you will cautiously consider the trust we place in you who read this. Don't rush right out to look. A swarm of people would be out of place in Orient. It also is a simple place; you won't be overwhelmed! The houses aren't as grand as those in Southampton or East Hampton. Property plots are rather small, and the antiques are not on a scale that would attract Sotheby's. It is not quaint, and there are no shops of any kind, other than a small general store and post office, closed Sunday. So you might be disappointed. But for us, Orient has a special character all its own.

If you go, you will leave Greenport on Route 25. The town of East Marion is 2 or 3 miles, and 3 miles beyond that, just after you cross the narrow causeway with the Long Island Sound on your left and Orient Harbor on your right, is the road (Village Lane) that leads down into the village. As you come to this causeway, you should stop at the parking place along the harbor, get out, and look. The map lays out well before you here. The village, from this distance, seems like one you'd see in Vermont. There are snowy white egrets that nest in the salt meadows and a peacefulness laid down on the whole scene. We have read that Orient until after World War I was a favorite spot for honeymooners. Today it is primarily a quiet resort town.

Don't try to drive into town. Park off the road near the war memorial obelisk and the white church with the graceful steeple, at the head of the lane. If you do drive through, note the NO PARKING signs that alternate from one side to the other. Then walk along the Village Lane sidewalk. Houses, gardens, trees, and reflections will catch your eye. Orient has more than one hundred buildings built more than a century ago. Down the quiet, narrow, meandering Village Lane are the Oyster Ponds Museums, a six-building museum complex that is run by the Oyster Ponds Historical Society (631–323–2480). The first building is the Village House Museum, a simple clapboard structure with a long widow's walk. It has Early American furnishings and local collections and is clearly worth a visit. Behind it is the Hallock House with marine art, artifacts, and tools. Next door is the Old Schoolhouse; across the street, the Webb House. Then there is the Red Barn, and so on.

The museum buildings are open on Saturday and Sunday from 2:00 to 5:00 P.M. the end of June through September, and also on Wednesday and Thursday in July and August. There is an admission fee.

After visiting the museum group, continue down the lane by the yacht club, and you can lengthen the walk as we do by continuing on out into the country fields and swinging back by a loop into the village.

Woodlands, Parks, and Preserves

The idea of finding a pleasant trail winding through quiet woods or open fields may seem hard to accept on this island of 2.6 million people in Nassau and Suffolk Counties, yet the reality is that there are miles and miles of such walks to be enjoyed. Only a few are listed in this section, forming a starting point for further exploration. They are mostly in fairly large areas that have been saved from being paved with roads and houses by state or county acquisition and/or by The Nature Conservancy. The woods, roads, and trails are used by walkers, horseback riders, cyclists, birders, and joggers as an escape from urban pressures, and they serve this purpose well. Other sections in this volume list similar walks; the ones here are primarily those where water is not a prominent part of the scene.

Many of these areas have extensive trail networks that offer a great deal of variety in the details you can observe as well as in the flora and fauna. Others have nature trails, usually self-guiding, that can provide more points of interest in a short distance than would be expected from simply wandering down an old road through a scrub oak woodland. In still others you'll find a long-distance trail passing through that, while interesting, doesn't lend itself to a loop walk to take you back to your starting point over new terrain. As a consequence, while we've highlighted the walks that seem best for first acquaintance, do try others that show on our maps or on the maps that are often available at the parks and preserves. We think you'll enjoy the variety, especially if you visit during different seasons of the year.

Garvies Point
Preserve and Museum

This sixty-two-acre area of glacial moraine has about 5 miles of marked nature trails over "the Carpenter Tract," purchased in 1668 from the Matinecock Indians. For thousands of years before this, woodland Natives had hunted, gathered, and camped on this and adjoining lands. The concentrated remains of their middens here are one of the reasons Nassau County acquired the land in 1963 and opened the museum, which specializes in Native American archaeology as well as regional geology. Physically Garvies Point is similar in many ways to the Sands Point Preserve (see Walk 29) on the opposite side of Hempstead Harbor. It acquired the name from a former owner, Dr. Thomas Garvie, who emigrated from Scotland to Glen Cove in the early nineteenth century. The preserve is open daily 8:30 A.M. to dusk, but the museum is only open Tuesday through Saturday from 10:00 A.M. to 4:00 P.M., and Sunday from 1:00 to 4:00 P.M. Admission to the museum is $2.00 for adults and $1.00 for children.

A parking area adjoins the museum. Exhibits give you a fine introduction to Long Island before its discovery by Europeans. There is a sweeping view of Hempstead Harbor as you stand here at the museum, and the nature trails that start here provide good walking any time of year.

Although in the midst of suburban neighborhoods, the high ridge along the shore may set your mind to wondering about the state of the Native People who stalked along it so many years ago. Those who greeted the settlers on Long Island were generally a congenial and helpful people and at first offered no resistance to the newcomers. Fish and game were plentiful, and they were adept at catching all that was needed. The northern climate here was ameliorated by the sea. Those early settlers recognized the advantages and were joined rather quickly by others who learned about the place. The history of these early days is well documented, and your local library may start you reading about these first encounters between the European settlers and the Native Americans.

During the warmer months the preserve is full of wildlife; the woods and meadows attract a great variety of birds. Because there's an effort to keep it in a natural state, a wide variety of native plants grow here. You'll find forty-eight species of trees, including northern red oak, pin oak, sassafras, beech, black cherry, persimmon, tulip tree, locust, sycamore, and butternut hickory. It is all in all a very pleasant experience to roam over these unexpected riches. There are 5 miles of trails, including a self-guided nature trail on Hempstead Harbor.

If you walk along the seashore, you can inspect the rocky beach and the bluffs above it. The sand contains the glacial debris so characteristic of all the North Shore. Only a few spots on Long Island, however, have glacial deposits so unusually thin as they are here at Garvies Point, thus exposing 70-million-year-old deposits of sand, silts, and multicolored clays. Well-preserved fossils of Cretaceous plants have even been found along these shorefront cliffs.

From the Long Island Expressway, the Northern State Parkway, Northern Boulevard, or the Meadowbrook Parkway, exit on Glen Cove Road, northbound. Continue on Glen Cove bypass (Route 107 north; keep left at the fork) to the last traffic light facing the Glen Cove Fire House. Turn right and follow signs to the museum (516–571–8010).

18

Muttontown Preserve

Under the stewardship of the Nassau County Museum, this 550-acre preserve combines the assets of a number of old North Shore estates to provide a quiet, rural, and startlingly extensive area for woodland walks. Situated in East Norwich south of Route 25A and west of Route 106, it is comprised of four principal areas, two of which are of primary interest to walkers.

The first of these is the fifty-acre Nature Center area, which features a marked self-guiding trail running through an irregular U-shaped parcel that largely surrounds one of the old mansions, Chelsea, which is now used for selected cultural exhibitions and affairs. The Bill Paterson Nature Center (516–571–8500) is at the end of Muttontown Lane, a little road running south off Route 25A in East Norwich. There is no fee for parking by the Nature Center in the preserve; the gate is open 9:30 A.M. to 4:30 P.M. daily. Behind the center is a little pond that was dug in 1967 to provide better drainage to the wet area here, and deciduous woods of swamp maple, pin oak, and tupelo, a tree closely related to the sourgum of southern swamps that turns scarlet in autumn. Although the pond doesn't support any fish, it does provide the environment needed by a variety of beetles and other insects and attracts turtles, frogs, and salamanders, as well as an assortment of birds.

Happily the trails are marked with colored number posts, and this is most helpful to guide you along twisty, turny paths where otherwise you might miss seeing much the area offers.

Many of the trees are marked, too, for identification. Watch out for poison ivy, which grows rankly throughout the preserve!

Follow the green markers for trail 1 through the swamp area where you will find arrowwood and spicebush growing, along with ferns, mosses, and liverworts. You will come out on a large field, once farmland, now let go so that it attracts bobwhites and pheasants, field mice and red foxes. Turn right here following the green blazes into the evergreen woods. On the hot summer day we walked here, the cool of these woods was noticeable. It is a forest of white pine and larch, with a scattering of dogwood and black cherry, and paths are spongy, so you stride forth with an easy gait.

Don't be upset if you lose your sense of direction. The path actually doubles back, and you find yourself turned around heading north on the green trail, which goes nearly back to Route 25A, before returning. Partway along you can cross over on the yellow marker (#4) if you prefer a shorter walk.

The other major area for walking is the contiguous 200-acre parcel south of the Nature Center trails down to Muttontown Road. The trails in this area are mainly bridle paths left over from the days when all this was horse country. They are mostly marked with colored and numbered posts as they wind through evergreen woods and open meadows, past glacially formed rolling hills and kettle-hole ponds. This section has its own parking area, entered from Route 106, about 1,000 feet north of the Muttontown Road intersection. This large lot is still actively used for horse trailers and supports both hikers and users of the equestrian practice areas.

This part of the preserve, along with 250 acres south of Muttontown Road that are not open for general use, comprised the Lansdell Christie Estate. Some overgrown ruins in the woods north of Muttontown Road are the only remaining evidence of a mansion there that was once owned (but never used) by King Zog of Albania.

If everyone who walks here comes as a guest and is concerned about and aware of the life preserved here, we shall have a treasured little sanctuary forever wild.

19

Uplands Farm Sanctuary

The Long Island chapter of The Nature Conservancy (516–367-3225) has its headquarters in farm buildings that are surrounded by open fields and upland woods on Lawrence Hill Road, in Cold Spring Harbor, about 0.25 mile east of the junction of Routes 25A and 108. There are trails through the preserve that not only visit varied terrain, but also connect with the Nassau-Suffolk Greenbelt Trail to permit a 2.25-mile loop walk. A detailed guide is available at the kiosk. The office is open weekdays 9:00 A.M. to 5:00 P.M., but the trails are open daily dawn to dusk. During office hours you can visit the Conservancy's library.

Though it is a national organization, The Nature Conservancy works quietly and most effectively on the local level, and the two chapters on Long Island have been responsible for the acquisition of more than seventy natural areas here, many of them ecologically fragile. The Sunken Forest on Fire Island (see Walk 2), the North Shore Wildlife Sanctuary, and a section of Caumsett State Park (see Walk 33) are all properties that The Nature Conservancy helped set aside for conservation purposes.

We have walked a number of these natural areas that belong to the Conservancy with great satisfaction, and they are open to serious walkers with permits. If interested, you should contact the organization directly.

20

Target Rock
National Wildlife Refuge

This interesting refuge is, like the Elizabeth A. Morton National Wildlife Refuge (see Walk 45), managed by the U.S. Fish and Wildlife Service to preserve endangered plants and animals, to preserve natural diversity, and to perpetuate migratory bird life. It covers eighty heavily wooded and rolling acres at the eastern end of Lloyd Neck and contains about 0.3 mile of beach on Huntington Bay south of Fort Point and Target Rock.

The refuge was once the estate of financier Ferdinand Eberstadt, who built a thirty-five-room neo-Georgian mansion there in 1937 on one of the higher points. After his death the property was deeded to the government in 1967 as a wildlife refuge. There is a 0.5-mile trail to the beach that goes through mature oak-hickory woods and passes close to a brackish pond that always has a few waterfowl in residence. In addition, a new wheelchair-accessible trail leads from the beach trail at the office through the woods to the open field that was the site of the old mansion. Access for wheelchair visitors is moderately difficult from the parking lot to the beginning of the nature trail. There is also a 0.25-mile side trail along the south side of the knob where the old mansion once sat. Along the trail is a grove of magnificent tall oaks.

The refuge is very popular with wildlife. All told, naturalists have identified more than 300 species of birds, mammals, reptiles, and amphibians in the Target Rock National Wildlife Refuge.

The trails are broad and easy to manage even as you stay on the lookout for wildlife; if you stay clear of grass at the beach, your risk of acquiring a tick should be minimal.

When you look north along the beach, you'll see two large boulders just offshore. They were once part of the glacial residue in the morainal bluff above them, but the land has eroded to the west to leave them in the bay. At the time of the American Revolution, the bigger one was still up in the bank, but exposed, so British warships offshore used it as a gunnery target—hence the name Target Rock.

The refuge is open daily, from half an hour before sunrise to half an hour after sunset. An information kiosk and public rest rooms are located at the headquarters area and are wheelchair accessible. Fishing from the beach is permitted. Watercraft are not allowed to land at the refuge.

You can reach the refuge from Huntington by following West Neck Road and Lloyd Harbor Road 2.2 miles past the entrance to Caumsett State Park. Questions? Call (631) 271–2409, or, if there's no answer, call the Long Island National Wildlife Refuge complex at (631) 286–0485.

There is a $4.00 entrance fee per car. Annual passes are available for $12.00, and free Golden Age/Access Passports for seniors and the disabled are also honored. These passes are distributed in person at both Target Rock and Wertheim Refuges (see Walk 24).

21

Caleb Smith
State Park Preserve

This 543-acre tract dates back to 1663, when the first Smith bought the land from the Indians. Smith ownership continued for more than 200 years until Caleb started selling parts of it to the Brooklyn Gun Club (later the Wyandanch Club). By 1900 the club had all the land and had completed its expansion of the original house to what you now see as the museum building. The property was bought by New York State in 1963 as part of a planned program of open-space preservation. It is now open for "passive" recreation as an environmental preserve with ponds, a number of trails that total more than 5 miles (including the Long Island Greenbelt and two self-guiding nature trails), and a modest museum in the imposing old clubhouse.

Park hours are 8:00 A.M. to sunset; it's open Wednesday through Sunday all year, and also on Tuesday, April through September. There is a $5.00 vehicle fee every day from April 1 to Labor Day, and on weekends only from Labor Day to March 21. In case you plan to walk through the part of the preserve that is south of Route 25 or to pass through the whole preserve on the Greenbelt, be sure to get the combination for the locked gate you will encounter when you enter or leave the preserve. The Long Island Greenbelt Trail Conference will tell you about the Greenbelt

CALEB SMITH
STATE PARK
PRESERVE

Meadow Road

PHILLIPS MILL
POND

W

W

25

Museum

W

★

NISSEQUOGUE RIVER

Blydenburgh State Park

WILLOW
POND

WEBSTER
POND

W

N

W

W

Old Willets Path

0   ¹/₁₀   ²/₁₀   ³/₁₀
Miles

Trail and give you the combination for the gate. Its phone number is (631) 360–0753. Call several days in advance; if no one is there, someone will get back to you. As a courtesy, you should also call the preserve at (631) 265–1054 to let the staff know you would like to visit. They will let you know when they are open and if all the trails are accessible. If you are interested, you should inquire about their nature programs. When you enter the parking area, you will see the Nature Museum to your left. The museum is well worth the visit. You will find knowledgeable people there; trail maps and a wide range of interpretive brochures are available.

The preserve is bisected by the Jericho Turnpike (Route 25), which runs in a curve southwesterly here. The entrance is off the northern side of the highway, 3 miles east of the Sagtikos State Parkway and 0.75 mile east of Old Willets Path. Be careful when turning into the parking area—this straightaway stretch of Route 25 encourages speeders!

One other survivor from colonial times (not open to the public) is the Aron Vail House, which was an inn on the old stagecoach route and a point of interest in early Smithtown history. On both sides of Route 25, the preserve is made up of swamp and upland and provides a fine habitat for many geese and ducks, a wide variety of birds, rabbits, raccoons, and native wildlife. We found the undulating trail soft and pleasant footing, remarkably quiet in one of the busiest sections of Suffolk County.

On our walk here we followed a number of trails blazed for cross-country skiing and stayed mostly on the northwest side of the preserve. These rolling slopes and hillsides are the northern side of the Ronkonkoma Moraine, and the drainage flows into the Nissequogue River, then Long Island Sound.

The part of the preserve south of Route 25, where the Nissequogue meanders through ponds and lowlands, was a mecca for fly fishermen when it was a private club. It is now open to the public on a strict reservation basis and still provides excellent fly-fishing.

22

Connetquot River
State Park Preserve

Connetquot River State Park Preserve is an ideal place to walk. It has a very special place in the Long Island state park system; the designated term *preserve* means that there are no ball fields or playgrounds or picnic areas. The idea is to keep an area like this much as it has always been and to limit its use to "passive recreation," such as walking, horseback riding, and fishing. Bicycles are not permitted here.

In order to keep the character of the preserve undisturbed, walkers are required to get a permit in advance. Write to Connetquot River State Park, P.O. Box 505, Oakdale, NY 11769, giving your name, your address, and the number of people in your party. The park is open year-round Wednesday through Sunday 8:00 A.M. to 4:30 P.M., and April 1 through Labor Day it is also open on Tuesday. Maps are available at the booth by the park entrance. There is a vehicle user fee of $5.00. If you have questions, call (631) 581–1005.

A word about getting to the preserve's obscure entrance off the Sunrise Highway, Route 27, which is a divided three-lane highway that has been under major reconstruction. You can enter Connetquot only from the westbound lanes, so if you are headed east, proceed past the park entrance about 1 mile to the Oakdale-Bohemia Road exit. Get off there, turn left over the bridge, and head west along the service road or right-hand lane to reach the park entrance. Look sharp for the white pavement markings of a very short exit lane.

An explanation of how an oasis this size, nearly 3,500 acres, is possible is in the deed, which was held by a syndicate of wealthy sportsmen as a private trout stream and hunting preserve for well over one hundred years. Before that it was held as a patent dating back to pre-Revolutionary times. When you leave your car at the parking lot and stroll out by the buildings near the entrance booth, you will be seeing what was the clubhouse and what has been available for public access only since 1973. In days gone by others who walked these trails whom you just might have heard of include Daniel Webster, Ulysses S. Grant, General Sherman, Lorenzo Delmonico, and Charles L. Tiffany, to name a few—membership was limited to one hundred names at any time.

We headed out on the red-blazed trail—there are miles and miles of trails, including a section of the north-to-south Long Island Greenbelt Trail—catching glimpses of the Connetquot River as we went along. It was late November and all the migrating birds had passed through, but we saw hooded mergansers, mallards, swans, and a female wood duck. We saw three deer and surprised two rabbits, a squirrel, and a fox.

"It was a red fox. We have them here," Gil Bergen, the park superintendent who has managed the place for many years, told us. "You are lucky to see one in the daytime."

On a recent spring visit, our day was made complete by a close encounter with a couple of wild turkeys, the tom in gorgeous multicolored display and the hen trudging slowly along behind. It was an uncommon and beautiful sight.

23

Three Parks with Views

To suggest climbing hills on Long Island may appear frivolous, but since we have an urge to reach heights and see the view from there, it occurs to us that others may, too. That's why we're suggesting these three morainal hills that command unusual views for this area. West Hills County Park boasts Jayne's Hill, at 401.5 feet above sea level the highest point on Long Island. Next comes Colonie Hill in Islip's Hidden Pond Park (180 feet), and then Bald Hill (285 feet) in Suffolk Hills County Park.

Jayne's Hill is in the northeast corner of West Hills Park, a heavily wooded area with an extensive network of blazed trails and woods roads that justify visiting it even without a view. The view is limited in width, but it is a fine outlook to the southwest, with the Atlantic, 13 miles away, easily seen on a clear day.

It's possible to drive nearly to the top of Jayne's Hill by finding Walt Whitman's old house off Route 110 in Melville (look for historic markers), and then going directly west from there (after a visit!) on West Hills Road; 3 blocks later, turn left onto Reservoir Road. This road rises steeply to end just below the top. Follow a footpath on the left side of the water tank to the high point and view.

If you'd like more exercise than this, head to the park office for a free copy of a detailed trail map. The office is on High Hold Drive. You can get there from the Jericho Turnpike (Route 25) by going south on Round Swamp Road 0.4 mile and turning left onto High Hold, or else try back roads west from Route 110. If

you then wish to explore the park or just hike up to Jayne's Hill, follow the map to reach Sweet Hollow Road and then go south on it to a parking and picnic area just beyond a big riding stable. By a variety of trails, Jayne's Hill is a bit more than a mile away.

The second lookout is Colonie Hill in Hauppage, where the Long Island Greenbelt Trail crosses the Ronkonkoma Moraine and passes through Hidden Pond Park. Here there are woodlands closely surrounded by "civilization," but the pleasant view north is won by a very short walk (less than 0.25 mile) from where the trail crosses the Motor Parkway. To get there, go east on the Motor Parkway from exit 57 of the Long Island Expressway (Route 495) to a point 1.2 miles beyond the intersection with Route 454. When you reach the point where some major high-tension lines cross overhead, stop and park. There is a gate in the north-side fence there, and a slim opening next to it where the white-blazed Greenbelt heads north. Follow it; when the trail turns west along the ridgeline, you'll find the views, and a couple of benches to help you enjoy them. The bulk of the park is down below on the north side of the moraine; parking is available there, too.

The final lookout, Bald Hill, is about 3.5 miles south of Riverhead just off Route 51. It's in an undeveloped county park, but close to the highway. Park your car off the road by the gate 0.6 mile south of where Route 51 and Speonk Riverhead Road split. Go in past the barriers and walk the heavily worn road directly away from the highway. Follow the blue-and-white rectangular blazes along a loop trail. You will visit a dense pine-oak woods. Then a steep climb will bring you to a fine view northeast through a gap in the pines. Peconic Bay, Robins Island, and Shelter Island will all be visible on a good day. This whole venture should take about an hour.

For another invigorating walk and climb, go left on Speonk Riverhead Road when you reach it from Riverhead. After 0.3 mile turn in at the entrance to Suffolk Community College. Take the first left then the first right into east parking field 1, then head for the northwest corner, where there is a fine, roofed map

and notice board. Park there and follow a clear but poorly maintained yellow-blazed nature trail roughly north to and along the
west edge of a big glacial kettle hole. At a junction with the white-
blazed Pine Barrens Trail (Paumanok Path), go left on it, cross
Route 51, and proceed southwest, parallel to Route 51. Continue
to follow the white rectangle blazes of the Paumanok Path and
you will easily find your way up the face of Bald Hill. This route
means a 3-mile round trip from your car over rolling terrain. On
a relatively flat island, this 300-foot-high panoramic view makes
the exertion well worthwhile.

You'll find many roads leading off into these woods. Extend
your walks and enjoy them while you can, but don't get lost—it's
easy to do in the pine barrens. In fact, if you're serious about exploring this area, we suggest you contact the Long Island Greenbelt Trail Conference (see p. xv) to get a copy of the Long Island
Pine Barrens Trail map or any other current offerings. U.S. Geo-
logical Survey maps are good, too, but are not nearly as complete or up to date with trail information.

24

Wertheim National Wildlife Refuge

Long Island has nine national wildlife refuges, one of which (Target Rock; see Walk 20) we have already covered. They all share the common goal of providing habitat for migratory and resident birds and for other indigenous wildlife. With the exception of Jamaica Bay (see Walk 36), which is administered separately, they are together managed by the Long Island National Wildlife Refuge Complex, centered at the Wertheim Refuge in Shirley (631–286–0485).

Wertheim is notable both for size (2,400 acres) and for the diversity of habitats it provides. About half are aquatic and half are uplands. A prominent feature is the Carmans River, a New York State–designated Wild and Scenic River. It is the second longest river on Long Island. The Carmans River estuary, which includes Bellport Bay, is the key to water-based life, since it varies in salinity from fresh to brackish to almost full saline in the bay. The estuary is complemented by extensive marshes, swamps, and marine grasslands. The upland areas are on a sandy glacial outwash plain, with pitch pine, oak-pine, and oak–red maple stands being dominant.

Diverse habitats lead to diverse inhabitants; at the Wertheim Refuge these include more than 240 species of birds. A high pro-

portion of the birds are migratory, and Wertheim is a favored stop on the Atlantic Flyway. Visitors will enjoy the excellent nature trail that covers 3 miles in a big loop starting at the refuge office, with a shortcut available in the middle that makes for a 1.5-mile loop. This White Oak Nature Trail has two blinds for viewing open field areas and waterways. Visitors are effectively hidden from being noticed by the birds and animals out in the open, yet have an unimpeded view of them.

The best seasons for viewing are difficult to define because of the great variety of species here. Migratory waterfowl are present in the greatest numbers October through April. Resident birds are most active during the day, as are the deer and wild turkeys, but the smaller animals favor dawn and dusk when the refuge may not be open. You can't really expect to have a lot of sightings in any one visit, but repeated visits should pay off. Trying different seasons and times should provide a good representation of Long Island's native flora and fauna.

The refuge is located on the South Shore of Long Island about 6 miles east of Patchogue. From the Long Island Expressway (Route 495, exit 68), go south on the William Floyd Parkway (Route 46) about 3 miles to the intersection directly *after* the exit from the Sunrise Highway. This is the Montauk Highway (Route 80). Turn right on it. Go about 1 mile and then turn left at the traffic light. Head south on Smith Road for about 0.3 mile (just after the railroad tracks) to the refuge entrance on your right. Follow the entrance road about 0.5 mile to the visitor parking area and information kiosk. Visiting hours are Monday through Friday 8:00 A.M. to 4:30 P.M. All visitors are asked to sign in at the kiosk. An excellent brochure is available there for the nature trail. For more information stop in the adjacent building, which serves as the headquarters of the Long Island National Wildlife Complex, or call (631) 286–0485. If you enjoy boating or fishing, inquire about the two boat-launch sites and nearby rental facilities.

SEARS-
BELLOWS
COUNTY
PARK

W = White Blazes
    Paumanok Path

BL = Blue Loop Trail

25

Sears-Bellows County Park

Sears-Bellows lies to the north of the Sunrise Highway (Route 27) and south of Flanders Road (Route 24), but fortunately has enough acreage to offer a feeling of remoteness, complete with two lakes, some ponds, and lots of cover for deer and game birds, including the marvelously colored wood duck. Walking here is most pleasant in spring or fall. People are essentially gregarious, we have observed, and like to be where the crowd is, enjoying the fishing and boating at the big lake, Bellows. Thus, even when we walk here in season, in a few easy strides away from the camping area you lose almost everyone.

You will find parking spaces here, as in all Suffolk County parks, limited in season to Suffolk County residents with permits. Trails are not heavy-traffic areas, and hikers are not discouraged, so if you do not have a permit, the park staff will treat you courteously if you are not a nuisance.

The park is open daily all year but may have shorter daily hours off season. An additional concern is that some areas in the park are open to hunting in midwinter, so before heading off into the woods in the November-through-January period, check with the park office (631–852–8290) for any restrictions or for park hours.

The best entry to the park is on Bellows Pond Road off Flanders Road (Route 24), 5 miles south of the Riverhead traffic circle and 1.8 miles from exit 65 on Route 27.

Many dirt roads make good paths through the woodlands and around the lakes, and if it is a quiet day when you come, the walk around Bellows Pond is an easy one. Our favorite walk, however, is from Bellows to Sears Pond. The paths are especially nice for walking, pine needles underfoot, mostly wide, and unobstructed. Go south of Bellows Pond first, then on the west side take a sharp left onto the recently defined Sears Pond Trail, whose blue blazes lead quite directly from the park entrance area to the pond. You will pass through the woods, where we always seem to flush out a grouse or two, past a pond on your right that is a favorite haunt of the wood duck, then swing left and into a clearing that has a significant rise of land on it. We usually climb the rise and sit for a few minutes, because there is often a red-tailed hawk here circling, and there is always a view of the surrounding country. We continue on the path on the other side of the hill and walk about a mile northwestward through sparse, burned-over woods. The growth and vegetation increase heavily as you come to Sears Pond. Go down to the water quietly; the ducks are wary in this secluded hideaway.

You should note that a few trails on the west side of the park have been set aside for the exclusive use of horse riders; they are closed to hikers and not shown on this map. While we hate to lose trails. this has to be a good move where dual use is heavy.

Although the muffled traffic noise from the two highways does carry across the treetops, Sears-Bellows is as free today of the sounds of our civilization as almost anywhere else.

The Paumanok Path crosses Route 24 just east of Red Creek Road. It is a short walk from the public parking areas on either side of Route 24 (located just west of Red Creek Road) to this crossover point. The Paumanok Path generally runs east–west, but at this point it connects two parks located north and south of each other. A walk to the south will take you to the blue-blazed loop trail that visits both Sears and Bellows Ponds. A walk north will take you to Hubbard Creek and Red Creek Park's Penny Pond.

26

Mashomack Preserve

Mashomack is unique. In its 2,000 acres of woodlands, marshes, and tidal creeks, it provides a greater variety of habitats and a greater variety of birds than any other area on Long Island. It occupies the southeastern third of Shelter Island, between the twin forks, and so can be reached only by a short ferry ride (South Ferry is closer and quicker than North Ferry). We are able to enjoy it only because it was purchased in 1980 by The Nature Conservancy from a farsighted family.

The feature most notable, other than the tremendous scenic beauty of the preserve, is its vastness. Walking on some of the 20 miles of trails here, it's hard to believe you are only 90 miles away from New York City. At Mashomack, together with protected areas to the south around Northwest Harbor, a maritime environment of unsurpassed richness has been given a fighting chance. The extensive salt marshes of the area are vitally significant as a breeding ground and nursery for organisms at the bottom of the food chain, upon which all other life depend.

Four well-marked trails offer hikes of varying lengths and difficulty, up to 11 miles. All of them start at the visitor center. On weekends and throughout the summer, staff and volunteer naturalists answer questions about the natural and human history of the preserve. The visitor center has a gift shop along with displays about The Nature Conservancy's work and the natural history of the East End. There is also a trail for the handicapped and visually impaired, featuring a wide variety of native plants. Wheelchairs, all-terrain strollers, and binoculars are available on loan here.

Mashomack can easily be reached from either north or south, because Route 114 connects with both ferries. The preserve entrance is on the east side of the road, 0.9 mile from the South Ferry. The visitor center is but a short walk from the parking area. It and the preserve are open daily from 9:00 A.M. to 5:00 P.M. May through September, and on weekends year-round, with a suggested donation of $2.00 for adults. For more information call (631) 749–1001.

The majority of the preserve is upland oak and beech forest, which includes a rare pine swamp complex, the only community of its kind known to occur on Long Island. There is almost no open water in this wetland, and all the plants are rooted in a floating mat of sphagnum moss. Because of its ability to retain many times its own weight in water, sphagnum moss plays an important part in keeping wetlands moist during dry periods.

An abundance of bird life makes Mashomack a paradise for ornithologists. Seventy-six breeding species have been recorded, and as many as fifty-six different species can be seen during winter at the preserve. To truly appreciate Mashomack, it is important to visit during all the seasons and at different times of the day. Spring is marked by the return of the first pairs of ospreys from South America. More than any other creature, they represent the wild spirit of Mashomack. They can be seen all along the shores plunging down for fish and circling triumphantly with their catch. Summer is when most visitors come, and a variety of guided walks (call for a schedule and to register) allow interpretive experiences ranging from an early-morning stroll filled with birdsong to a watery wade through a tidal creek.

In autumn hundreds of black ducks, Canada geese, and other migrating birds stop over at Mashomack. This is one of the best times for bird-watching, for the fall foliage provides a backdrop of exploding colors: the scarlet of red maple and sweet gum, golden beech leaves, red dogwoods, and orange bittersweet.

Winter offers great opportunity for tracking deer, foxes, and even mink. Harbor seals can be found basking on rocks in Gardines Bay in the winter sun.

27

Hither Hills State Park

The Hither Hills area contains a 1,755-acre state park and two preserves totaling 1,340 acres. They come at the east end of the long, narrow finger of land that connects the prehistoric Montauk Island with the south fork at Amagansett. The state park includes the long, sandy triangle that is the eastern shore of Napeague Harbor, the western half of the morainal upland, and about 1.3 miles of ocean and campground to the south. The balance of the upland, extending a bit over 2 miles along the north side of the Montauk Parkway (Route 27), contains two contiguous preserves. The whole area has many sand roads and trails in the mixed pine-oak forest, and natural features and wildlife that make it attractive to the walker.

When you first arrive here, make a point of stopping for a few minutes at the overlook on Route 27, on your left as you reach the highest level of the moraine (the second crest). Leave your car to survey the panorama and get oriented. In the foreground you'll find an area that was decimated in a 1986 forest fire, and is now recovered but not quite a forest yet. Beyond it you have a good view of Napeague Harbor, with the Atlantic on your left, and the southwest end of Block Island Sound and Gardiners Island to your right. This is also a good central place to park while you explore the park and preserves (no parking along Route 27, technically a parkway).

Be certain to visit the two information kiosks located at the overlook. The one located at the eastern corner always has a supply of complimentary trail maps and interpretive brochures. There is a great deal to see here; a visit to the kiosks will help you structure your experience.

The western triangle has the harbor shore on the west, a long beach facing Block Island Sound on the north, and wooded uplands on the east. There are two areas to visit here that you will enjoy. The first is the Walking Dunes, an interesting group of sand hills that are very gradually creeping across the flat terrain in response to prevailing northwest winds. As they move, they gradually cover the trees in their path, while the trees respond by growing taller. It's probably a draw most of the time. The advancing face of the dunes is beautifully rounded and smooth, while there's a nice view from the dune crest. To find the dunes, head north on Napeague Harbor Road, which is off Route 27 just west of the Hither Hills State Park boundary. Continue over the Long Island Rail Road crossing and proceed straight north to the end of the pavement, about 0.75 mile. Park on the side of the road where there is an information kiosk at the start of the nature trail. Get a Walking Dunes leaflet and set off east on the trail. You'll be on the side of a steep dune in only a few hundred feet. Ill-defined paths through the trees and underbrush to your right will enable you to climb up the side without too much fuss, but do avoid disturbing the advancing face of the dunes.

The route to Goff Point is obvious along the harbor shore, but for an easier path, follow the shore for only a few hundred yards beyond the pavement until there's a gap in the sand bank on your right. Go through the gap; you will soon find a firm interior sand road that makes for easy walking either to the point or to the northern shore.

Another nice place to visit is Fresh Pond, a favorite for fishing, bird-watching, and viewing other animals. This large pond can be reached by walking south from the overlook. It can also be accessed from the west on the newly cut portion of the Paumanok Path, which crosses over Napeague Harbor Road a short distance south of the Walking Dunes. Look for the white-and-blue trail emblem and white rectangle on a telephone pole on the east side of the road. Keep in mind that when you park, all four tires must be off the road to avoid being ticketed. Be on the lookout for poison ivy.

The two preserves that lie to the east of the state park begin where the power lines head northeast and downhill from Route 27, a short distance east of the overlook. They offer several miles of woods roads, easy trails, and bayside bluffs. To visit these preserves, the best place to park is at the entrance to the town recycling center, 2 miles east of the overlook on Route 27. Park just off the highway on the shoulders of the road leading to the recycling center, between the gate and Route 27. The parkway trail crosses this section of road.

Your enjoyment of the Hither Hills area will be greatly enhanced if, before you arrive there, you buy two very useful items. One is an excellent Hither Hills trail map that you can get from the town clerk at the East Hampton town offices, at 159 Pantigo Road (Route 27). It is the key to not getting lost in the woods! The other is the *South Fork–Shelter Island Preserve Guide* issued by The Nature Conservancy, P.O. Box 5125, East Hampton, NY 11937. It's an excellent seventy-five-page booklet that tells you a great deal about thirty-one preserves in the south fork areas east of Southampton. It has details on how to find each preserve, trail directions, and what is interesting about each from a naturalist's viewpoint.

The park and preserves are open daily, without charge, all year. You should know, however, that hunting is permitted at various times in the park during late fall and winter. We suggest you call the park office at (631) 668–2554 for a tape, (631) 668–2461 April through November, or (631) 668–5000 during winter to find out the exact dates of the open seasons for various types of game. Another good source of information is the New York State Department of Environmental Conservation in Stony Brook (631–444–0273), which issues the necessary hiking permits.

Former Estates

In the era beginning about 1900 and extending through the 1920s, literally hundreds of wealthy people bought tracts of land on Long Island to create estates for themselves. The favored areas were along the shores of the sound and in the gentle hills of Nassau and western Suffolk, north of main arteries like the Jericho Turnpike and the railroad. It is estimated that at least 500 major properties were acquired and mansions built on this Gold Coast, surely a unique suburban concentration.

Today, however, it is a different story. Population pressure and financial problems have resulted in most of the estates being broken up, mansions being demolished, and more modest homes being built (many still costing in the millions) in the spaces thus freed. A few of the big houses were acquired by schools, colleges, religious institutions, and various other public groups. In some cases the land remains undisturbed but the mansion has vanished, as you will note from some of the walks in this section. In others the mansion remains essentially unchanged and competes with the landscaped grounds for your attention.

This pattern of dividing and altering estates holds for all but one, Blydenburgh. It had remained, until 1938, under the ownership of a single family since colonial times. As a result, the house is not grand, but it has a fine setting overlooking the pond and mill that brought the owners their prosperity.

If you are intrigued by these estates, as we were, you might like to visit your library to read an elegant volume by Monica Randall titled *Mansions of Long Island's Gold Coast.* It has descriptions and photographs of a generous cross section of these estates, of their owners, and of their fates. It's a fascinating book.

28

U.S. Merchant
Marine Academy

Although fenced and entered through a guarded gate, the U.S. Merchant Marine Academy in Kings Point is open to the public daily from 8:00 A.M. to 4:30 P.M., and the eighty-two-acre grounds, formerly the estate of automobile magnate Walter P. Chrysler, make for a pleasant visit. The young American men and women who have the good fortune to get their education at this beautiful place should count themselves lucky in many ways. They have a stunning 180-degree view of Long Island Sound—the daintily soaring spans of the Throgs Neck and Whitestone Bridges and the cubes and rectangles of Manhattan. The campus includes docks with an impressive variety of boats used by officers-in-training to gain the experience necessary to handle any kind of vessel.

There are three buildings that deserve a visit, all on the bluff overlooking the sound and waterfront. To the south is the handsome Memorial Chapel; near it the white administrative center (Wiley Hall), the home of Walter P. Chrysler for many years; and at the north end, the American Merchant Marine Museum. It features a history of the academy, an exceptionally fine collection of more than fifty ship models, and other memorabilia. The curator is Frank Braynard, the noted marine author, artist, and lecturer. The museum (516–773–5515) is open Tuesday through Friday 10:00 A.M. to 3:00 P.M., and Saturday and Sunday 1:00 to 4:30 P.M., but it is closed from the last weekend of June to the first weekend of August and on federal holidays.

The academy is located on Steamboat Road, facing Long Island Sound, and a circuit of the campus makes an interesting, easy walk. If they appeal to you, you may watch regimental reviews some Saturday mornings in spring and fall (516–773–5000).

As for the training here, it is 100 percent science and engineering. The graduate achieves a bachelor of science degree, a U.S. Coast Guard license as a third mate or a third assistant engineer, and a commission as ensign in the U.S. Naval Reserve. There is no tuition. The ages of the students range from seventeen to twenty-five. The daily routine begins at 6:10 A.M., with classes from 8:00 A.M. to noon and 1:30 to 5:00 P.M.; lights off at 11:00 P.M. The school offers independent study and sea training on board merchant vessels. Two graduates from the class of 1942 who chose other careers after spending their early years at sea are J. Lane Kirkland, former president of the AFL-CIO, and Dr. Thomas Nicholson, who became director of the American Museum of Natural History.

29

Sands Point Preserve

Comprised of 216 acres of prime Long Island real estate, Sands Point Preserve stands on splendid bluffs overlooking Long Island Sound at the mouth of Hempstead Harbor, just north of Port Washington. For walkers it has six short, blazed trails and a small pond on land that supports a surprisingly wide range of plants and bird life. There is a mile of beachfront to explore as well. It is said that geologists find much of interest along here, in case you have rockhounding tendencies. In the wooded areas there are native trees that were here when the first settlers arrived and also specimen Oriental varieties that were brought in at the turn of the twentieth century.

No doubt these acres were groomed and manicured when the Goulds and then the Guggenheims lived here, but they are wilder now. There are two old manor houses and a large structure built to resemble a castle—Ireland's Kilkenny Castle, in fact—but to serve as a stable. Today this building houses special traveling exhibits on natural history, the visitor center, and the museum shop.

The two mansions, one (Hempstead House) built by the Gould family, were subsequently owned by the Guggenheims. Harry Guggenheim, who was an early flying enthusiast and admirer of the young Charles A. Lindbergh, built the other (Falaise) in 1923. Harry's home was the scene of many gracious social

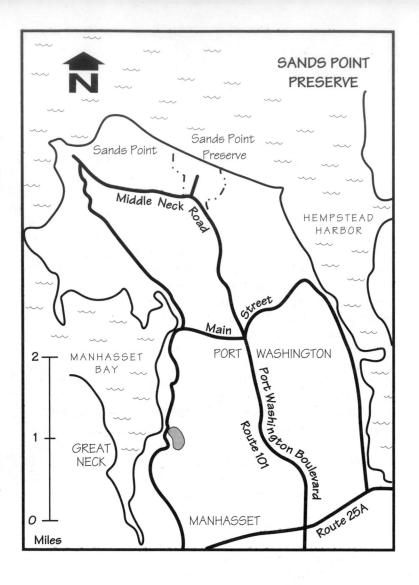

gatherings, for he was an outgoing man with many influential friends. When Lindbergh completed his historic flight across the Atlantic and returned to America, he was hard pressed to find any escape from the mobs that awaited him everywhere he went. Harry Guggenheim gave him sanctuary at Falaise. The strong friendship that developed between these two, the worldly and sophisticated older man and the inexperienced, shy young flier, is a remarkable story, too long to tell here.

Since Sands Point is an easy commute to New York and yet presents the aura of gracious country living together with access to the water and fine water views, the private homes out here tend to be large, protectively landscaped, and expensive. So it is indeed a privilege to have this fine old estate open to the public.

Since Falaise can be seen only on an escorted tour, you'll need to plan ahead. It is a comfortable and cozy Norman French country house, well worth a visit, and it shows the owners' gracious lifestyle. Conducted hourly, tours require reservations and an extra cost beyond the admission fee to the preserve ($2.00 weekends only in July and August). They're conducted in the afternoons; children under twelve are not permitted.

Hempstead House is also an exhibit building, featuring more than 2,000 pieces of Wedgwood ceramics (the Buten Collection), with a fee.

The preserve is managed by the Nassau County Department of Recreation and Parks. Because of financial belt tightening, its museum is not normally open in winter, though the grounds remain open without charge. In general, the museum season runs February through October, with some special exhibits scheduled at other times during the year. There are usually extra fees for the special exhibits. Daily hours are from 10:00 A.M. to 5:00 P.M.; closed Monday. For information on current events, specific museum/exhibit hours, and for Falaise tour reservations (afternoons only), call (516) 571–7900.

Of course, if antiques leave you cold, the trails and grounds alone should justify a visit. Stop at the visitor center for a trail map, and enjoy nature.

30

Nassau County Museum of Art

It wouldn't surprise us if William Cullen Bryant had been sitting on the very site of today's Nassau County Museum of Art when he wrote:

> *To him who, in the love of Nature, holds*
> *Communion with her visible forms, she speaks*
> *A various language.*

This was once his farmland, and he loved wandering over it. Today nature's visible forms still show themselves in nice variety, and a walk here is a quieting experience, even though it lies just off the busy thoroughfare of Northern Boulevard.

The Nassau County Museum of Art now occupies an imposing Georgian mansion on the hilltop that was last owned by the son of Henry Clay Frick, a cofounder of U.S. Steel. He lived there for nearly fifty years and did much to improve the main building and the surrounding 145 acres (with beautiful vistas) of woodland, ponds, and meadow. He had an active interest in nature, kept a variety of animals and birds, and planted a fine pinetum that still survives. The property was bought by Nassau County after his death in 1965, and the main house was converted to its present use after that.

The museum is well worth visiting to see the changing special exhibitions, which are the primary attractions. Predominantly keyed to modern art, they offer interesting views into many facets of the art world. It is good to phone before visiting, since the museum proper is usually closed for brief periods while a new exhibit is hung. The grounds, of course, are always open, and the best introduction to them is by first walking the perimeter road (a 1-mile loop) to get the lay of the land. Then explore the open fields and informal paths through the woods. There are no marked trails, but you should visit the pinetum as well as the formal garden next to the parking lot. On the northwest side of the grounds, you may spot a striking Gothic Revival cottage that Bryant had built in 1862 (now being restored).

One striking feature of the area is the presence of more than thirty modern sculptures in natural settings throughout the grounds. Some were commissioned, others are on extended loan, but all provide an interesting contrast to the parklike background. Be sure to get a "sculpture map" at the museum to guide you.

Just east of the parking lot you will find the new Tee Ridder Miniatures Museum. This fascinating exhibit includes twenty-six miniatures rooms, a Neoclassical doll house, and other exhibits of miniature art.

Do walk through the pinetum. It is more than just a shady place to stroll. In its heyday under Mr. Frick, it had more than 190 species of conifers, making it one of the best collections in America. Today it is mature and less exceptional, but it is still interesting and instructive to walk down the central corridor to see the seven species groups (firs, pines, hemlocks, spruces, yews, cypresses, and cedars). A leaflet with more details should be available at the museum.

The museum entrance is clearly marked on Northern Boulevard (just east of the railroad overpass at the top of the rise from the Roslyn Village area). From the Long Island Expressway, take exit 39 N (Glen Cove Road north) 2 miles. Turn left onto Route 25A. After two traffic lights, turn right onto Museum Drive. There is ample free parking. It is open Tuesday through Sunday from 11:00 A.M. to 5:00 P.M. Admission to both museums is $4.00 for adults, less for seniors and students. There is a pleasant small cafe in one wing, though you might be tempted to bring a sandwich to enjoy on a hillside near the woods. Museum information? Call (516) 484–9338.

31

Old Westbury Gardens

Long Island is fortunate that of the 500 Gold Coast estates that were built on the North Shore between 1900 and 1925, two of the very best remain for us to enjoy—Old Westbury Gardens and Planting Fields Arboretum (see Walk 32). Both have gracious mansions and superb landscapes and gardens that we can envy and perhaps try to copy. Both are large enough in area and diverse enough in their features to allow strolling about, continually discovering new aspects to admire.

On balance, we're inclined to prefer Old Westbury Gardens. Built in 1906 by John S. Phipps, American financier and sportsman, for his English wife, Margarita Grace Phipps, and their children, it is listed in the National Register of Historic Places. Its 150 acres include magnificent linden and beech allées, several ponds, and eight formal English gardens that are a tribute to the taste of George Abraham Crawley, the London-born designer of both the mansion and gardens.

You enter Old Westbury Gardens through magnificent eighteenth-century wrought-iron gates and drive through a towering allée of linden trees. After parking you can choose your own path or use the map you received at the entrance booth to embark on a 1.3-mile self-guided tour that could take up to two hours. Following the map, you are directed to the Boxwood Gardens, with a reflecting pool and classical Corinthian colonnade

OLD WESTBURY GARDENS

Rest Rooms

Ghost Walk

Walled Garden

Pinetum

Autumn Walk

Rose Garden

Temple of Love

Demonstration Gardens

EAST LAKE

Lilac Walk

Cottage Garden

Primrose Path

Linden Allee

Woodland Walk

Lake Trail

Shell Mosaic

Mansion

WEST POND

Gift Shop

Boxwood Gardens

0   1/10   2/10

Miles

N

Picnic Area and Cafe Rest Rooms

Parking Area

Entrance

that features a terra-cotta statue of Diana the Huntress flanked by huge, century-old weeping beeches. Continuing along the path down the Lilac Walk (in full bloom and deliciously fragrant in mid-May), you will pass through an exquisitely detailed wrought-iron gate into the two-acre Italian-style Walled Garden, which features an ever-changing display of blooming bulbs, shrubs, trees, perennials, flowering vines, ornamental grasses, annuals, and green lawns. The terracing, balustrades, summerhouses, lotus and lily pool (filled with flashing koi and goldfish), and pergola that supports aged but still-vigorous Chinese and Japanese wisteria all speak of its Italian design. But the kaleidoscope of blooming tulips, pansies, English daisies, delphiniums, swagged roses, both herbaceous and tree peonies, irises, phlox, Japanese anemones, chrysanthemums, dahlias, and so much more provides a reason to visit often throughout the season. When you leave the Walled Garden through its east gate, you can follow the Ghost Walk, lined with hedged hemlocks, past the English-style Pinetum into the formal Rose Garden. Patterned after seventeenth-century parterres in a complex pattern of interlocking circles and squares, the Rose Garden is planted with fragrant pink tea roses. A locustwood trellis that surrounds the garden and continues up the Primrose Path supports climbing and rambling roses of white, yellow, peach, rose, coral, and red. Near the top of the Primrose Path, the walk branches off to the right and provides a glimpse of the small thatched-roof Cottage with its own lovely garden—built as a playhouse for the Phippses' only daughter, Peggie. If you continue across the South Allée into the Demonstration Gardens area, you can visit a shade garden filled with shy blooms and sparkling variegated foliage plants, a daylily garden that peaks in July and August, the formal Grey Garden with drought-tolerant plants in full sun, the shady Green Garden that features a relaxing and cool color scheme, a vegetable garden to tempt the most demanding palate, several beautiful mixed borders, and an American Rose Society All-America test rose garden. From the Demonstration Gardens you can follow the path past the beautifully maintained swimming pool to walk around East Lake. The landscape around the lake is an ever-changing parade of flowering bulbs, native and exotic flowering trees and shrubs, a charming wooden bridge, and the Temple of Love—a romantic stone gazebo with a lacy wrought-iron roof that offers a smashing view of the house reflected in the still water of the lake. On the north bank follow the hillside Woodland Walk, which is at its best in early spring when ephemeral bulbs and wildflowers are in bloom. There is much more to see—vistas, statuary, and grand allées and hedges of beeches, hemlocks, and lindens stretch 0.5 mile to the north and south of the mansion.

At any time you can stop to tour the stately, terra-cotta brick mansion, built in seventeenth-century Charles II style. The designs of the house and the gardens are completely integrated—each is half of a perfect whole.

When you enter the mansion, you will see that there are fresh flowers in all the rooms, and that the dinner table is set, as though the Phipps family have just stepped out but are expected back shortly. The rooms are pleasant—light, airy, welcoming, and tastefully decorated, illustrating the gracious lifestyle that John S. Phipps and his family enjoyed. Although the home is not ostentatious, it displays evidence of considerable wealth—English antique furniture and decorative objects, gilded mirrors, crystal chandeliers, and fine paintings by Reynolds, Raeburn, Gainsborough, Constable, and Sargent. Each room contains original furnishings, arranged just as they were during the more than fifty years that Mr. and Mrs. Phipps and their four children lived here.

Old Westbury Gardens can be reached easily from the Long Island Expressway. Take exit 39 south and follow the service road east 1.2 miles to Old Westbury Road. Turn right and head south 0.25 mile to the entrance. The gardens are open Wednesday through Monday from 10:00 A.M. to 5:00 P.M. late April through October, and also in December for special holiday events in the mansion. There is an $8.00 admission fee to visit the grounds; admission to the grounds with a mansion tour is $10.00. Members enter free. Besides a gift shop in the mansion and a plant shop near the parking lot, you'll find special events (antique auto shows, English Country Fair, Scottish Games, and more), Talks & Tours with Master Gardeners, garden demonstrations by the professional horticultural staff, musical presentations (including music in the gardens, classical concerts in the Red Ballroom, and Picnic Pops in July and August), lectures, and symposia among the many events offered throughout the season. For more information call (516) 333–0048 or visit the Web site www.oldwestburygardens.org.

Other amenities include a picnic area (no fires) and the rustic Cafe in the Woods, which serves delicious light lunches and treats. All in all, Old Westbury Gardens is a place to visit again and again, ever fresh and lovely.

32

Planting Fields Arboretum

Planting Fields Arboretum State Historic Park is one of the most loved places on Long Island's Gold Coast, because it appeals to so many interests. The 409 acres of woodlands, trails, rolling lawns and fields, and cultivated gardens provide a wonderful setting for the Tudor Revival Coe Hall mansion, greenhouses, and other historic buildings. The entire property is listed on the National Register of Historic Districts.

In truth, the mansion and the landscaping compete as equals for the visitor's applause, thanks to the vision of William Robertson Coe. He bought the lands and the first house on the estate in 1913, and in 1918 began to build the present sixty-five-room mansion in a style of architecture reflecting what was popular during the reign of Queen Elizabeth I. Outstanding craftsmanship and meticulous detailing can be seen in hand-carved chimneys, stonework, and woodwork. The period rooms are fully restored and reflect a gilded age of grace and luxury. Coe Hall is open for guided tours April through September. The tours run from noon until 3:30 P.M. The fees for the tours are $5.00 for adults, and $3.50 for seniors; children age 7 to 12 are $1.00, and those under 7 are free. For more information call (516) 922–9210.

For the walker, 200 acres of historic landscape can be explored. Designed by the Olmsted brothers from 1918 to 1944, the arboretum offers a spectacular display of trees and shrubs, many imported. The sweeping lawns boast majestic beech and linden trees, as well as cedar, fir, elm, tulip, maple, holly, oak, and magnolia. Beyond the lawns and formal gardens are native fields and forest, with laurel, rhododendron, and dogwood prominent along the drives and trails.

Specialized garden areas and shrub plantings, including rose, dwarf conifer, rhododendron, and synoptic gardens, as well as extensive annual, perennial, and bulb plantings, provide inspiration and information for the gardener. Then there is the magnificent Main Greenhouse for specialized collections and seasonal displays, such as poinsettias and Easter lilies. The Camellia Greenhouse contains the largest collection of camellia trees in the Northeast.

There are many different ways to enjoy Planting Fields Arboretum; simply wandering at will across the lawns, through the gardens, and along 7 miles of woodland paths will give you numerous options to explore. Practically every area and season has something to offer.

Planting Fields is managed by the New York Office of Parks, Recreation, and Historic Preservation and is open every day of the year (except Christmas) from 9:00 A.M. to 5:00 P.M. The greenhouses are open from 10:00 A.M. to 4:00 P.M. Admission to the grounds is $5.00 per car all year on weekends and holidays, and on weekdays between May 1 and Labor Day. Volunteer opportunities at both the grounds and the museum are available. To reach Planting Fields, turn north off Route 25A onto Wolver Hollow Road, following it until it ends at Chicken Valley Road. Turn right, follow Chicken Valley Road for just over 2 miles, and then turn right again (shortly after you pass the magnificent Carshalton wrought-iron gates) onto Planting Fields Road to the entrance. Be sure to check out the Web site: www.plantingfields.org.

33

Caumsett State Park

Since 1961, 1,500 acres of the original 1,750-acre estate that made up the fabulous English-style domain of Marshall Field III has been owned by New York State. It sits at the head of a scenic peninsula jutting into Long Island Sound. Today it is administered by the Long Island State Park and Recreation Commission, and it's a grand place to walk.

A grand place in every way, because there are not apt to be crowds, with the many restrictions—no picnicking facilities (so you must pack your sandwich, bring your own drinking water, carry away your leftovers), no swimming, no pets, no playgrounds, no camping, and no driving beyond the parking area at the park booth, a matter of 2 miles to Long Island Sound.

This gives Caumsett a wonderfully remote aspect once you walk beyond the marvelous old farm buildings and magnificent stable nearby or down along the shore, so plan to spend the better part of a day. It is open Memorial Day through Labor Day from 8:00 A.M. to 4:30 P.M. daily. The entrance fee is $5.00 per car. To get there from Route 25A in Huntington, turn north onto West Neck Road to the park, a very pretty 5.5 miles.

It is hard to imagine that one man owned this vast park and that it was a farm that made its own power and was self-sufficient in almost every way. Miles of roads were built for motoring and horseback riding. There was tennis, indoors and out, pheasant

CAUMSETT
STATE PARK

LONG ISLAND SOUND

Marshall
Field
House

1

½

0

Miles

Riding
Stables

Dairy
Farm

★ Winter
Cottage

Summer Cottage

West Neck /
Lloyd Harbor Road

Park
Entrance

Henry Lloyd
House

LLOYD HARBOR

N

and skeet shooting, polo, trout fishing, a herd of prize cattle, and an extensive vegetable garden. None of the buildings is open to the public. They now house the Queens College Center for Environmental Teaching and Research, the BOCES Outdoor and Environmental Education Program, the Caumsett Equestrian Center, et cetera.

You will find here many specimen trees of interest—beech, oak, pine, dogwood, locust. You will find meadows, a salt marsh, and, below the large terrace of the main house, a pond where various waterfowl may be observed, and also the extensive shoreline along the sound. In winter there is a good chance of seeing rare Arctic seabirds at the pond or along the shore.

On the 27 miles of trails, there is hiking, jogging, and bicycling (helmets required). A limited number of permits is available for scuba diving and sound fishing. You'll also find cross-country skiing and bridle trails (although there are no rentals); you can make reservations for nature walks. For more information call the park office at (631) 423-1770.

34

Blydenburgh County Park

East of Old Willets Path, this Suffolk County park has had a long history with very few owners. In 1798 Isaac Blydenburgh, seeing a good business opportunity, joined with some Smith relatives to buy the 588-acre parcel. They put in the dam that created the pond and erected grist-, saw-, and fulling mills, which flourished for a long time. Blydenburgh became the sole owner in 1801, erected the present house in 1821, and passed the property on to his heirs. In 1938 the property left the family to become David Weld's estate, and he in turn sold it to the county in 1968.

The park is mostly woodland with swamps and fields, and is home to Stump Pond, which we understand is second in size on Long Island only to Lake Ronkonkoma. The pond is long and irregularly shaped, somewhat like a boot with a pointed toe. No swimming is permitted, but rowboats are available, so it is a popular fishing place as well as campground. A number of trails and dirt roads make for easy walking; you'll also encounter horseback riders.

The park has two focal points for visitors. One is on the north side of Stump Pond, where the old homestead and mill are located, and the other is at the south end. Both have parking and limited visitor facilities, and they connect with each other by trails along both sides of the lake. The park is open dawn to dusk; the park office is near the south entrance (631–854–3713). The best way to reach the northern part is from the western edge of the Smithtown Branch on Route 25, Jericho Turnpike. Turn south off the turnpike at the traffic signal at Brooksite Drive and go 1 block, then turn west onto New Mill Road, which leads directly into the park. The other part is reached from the Veterans Highway (Route 454) just across from the road leading to the county buildings south of the highway.

Parking is limited in season to Suffolk County residents with permits. At other times of the year, this restriction has not been rigorously enforced, and the chances are that the rangers will treat you with courtesy if you're not a nuisance.

Our suggestion for a good walk here is to follow the trail from the house by the north parking area down to Stump Pond. The trees near the house have all been planted but are native to the area. Once all this was tended farmland, but it was allowed some time ago to go back to nature. Now plants and surrounding shore are slowly filling in the lake, and it is all becoming overgrown. The area covered by the lake is 120 acres, and the fish consist of bass, sunfish, bluegills, as well as a few trout. The plants are common water lily and yellow pond lily, as well as water milfoil. You continue on the path southward across the dam by the mill and along the western shores of the lake to the stream, which you follow until the trail splits. Take the fork to your left, which crosses the stream and goes up the hill, and then follow it back so that you reach the high bluff of the peninsula from which you can see a whole panorama of the lake. The walk to this point is a little more than a mile, and if you wish to extend it, you can continue along the fire road toward the southern reaches of the lake.

The trail soon turns away from the lake to come out on Croft Lane. Turn left here and continue on south, passing through a strip of woodland. Then go left just north of some county buildings, and downhill to cross a footbridge over the south inlet brook and on to a connection with the east shore trail at the park office. A complete circuit around Stump Pond is a good workout, since it is nearly 5 miles long, but it abounds with lovely views of the lake and its numerous waterfowl.

35

Bayard Cutting Arboretum and Heckscher State Park

Anyone familiar with New York's Central Park knows the genius of Frederick Law Olmsted in grouping trees together. See what he started here on the banks of the Connetquot River on a very rich man's estate in 1886. There are 690 acres with trim lawns and open meadows, a wildflower garden, a marshy refuge, and paths that lead everywhere. Along the river's edge, around and through woods—it is difficult to imagine a nicer walk anywhere or one with a setting more gracious than the one provided for public use here. The estate is maintained by the Long Island State Park and Recreation Commission, given in trust to the state by Mr. Cutting's daughter. There is no picnicking, sports, or pets. There is a $5.00-per-car admission charge early April through Labor Day and on weekends up to the last weekend in October. Hours are 10:00 A.M. to sunset Tuesday through Sunday (631–581–1002).

To reach the arboretum, take the Southern State Parkway to the Heckscher Parkway. Leave it at exit 45E and follow the signs east along the Montauk Highway (Route 27A). Or take the LIRR to Great River Station; the arboretum is a 0.75 mile walk from the station.

There are five different trails laid out and marked, each with different colors, and were you to take the allotted time on each, the total time suggested would be three and a half hours. We recommend that you plan to spend at least two and a half hours

here and make a most pleasant morning or afternoon of it by combining two or more of these walks into one longer one.

There is also a seasonal aspect to consider in planning your walk here. Wildflowers should be out in late March and April, rhododendrons in late May and June. Changing colors are engaging in October. Even on a hot summer's day, however, the welcome release is here: A cooling breeze off the river, shade from the mature trees, and benches conveniently at hand will probably quietly lure you to sit a spell.

The rambly, old, informal house is partially open. Tea and simple snacks are available in season, cafeteria-style, and tables on the large, enclosed porch looking out over the river offer an attractive setting for a relaxing break.

Heckscher State Park has sandy beaches for swimming and a fine view of Great South Bay. It does, however, have a lot of wildlife in its interior. Naturally the deer, foxes, pheasants, wild turkeys, and other animals head for quiet areas in the populous peak of the day, but as sunset nears they get active again and more visible.

The Long Island Greenbelt Trail starts at the east end of parking field 8 on the edge of Great South Bay. (If field 8 is closed, use the unnumbered field to the west of it. There is a concrete walkway connecting these two fields.) It can provide a pleasant shore, meadow, and woods walk for whatever distance time and energy permit. In fact, after about 4 miles it passes "just across the road" from the entrance to the arboretum.

Heckscher Park is heavily used in summertime, but its nearly 1,700 acres can soak up a lot of people, and with the usual cool onshore breeze from the bay, it can still be a lovely place. There are wildflowers in the wetlands and meadows in spring, and in fall monarch butterflies pass through in great numbers as they migrate south. The park is open daily from 8:00 A.M. to sunset and is reached simply by following the Heckscher Parkway extension of the Southern State Parkway to the end. In summer months there is a $7.00 charge per car, in the "shoulder" months (April, May, September, October) it's $5.00, and at other times free. This park is handicapped accessible.

Marshes, Creeks, and Bogs

These aren't necessarily walks where you'll need your rubber foot gear, but water figures prominently in each. It may be a lake or marsh that is full of birds to be observed, or it may be a brook or nascent river heading for the sea with a trail beside it that leads you through lush undergrowth or giant trees. In any case there will be a lot more visible life here than is common in the drier woodland walks. That of course carries with it the prospect of mosquitoes in season and muddy spots on the trails here and there. We've found these drawbacks unimportant compared to the larger pleasures of these walks.

These wetlands, and of course the ocean and sound beaches, reveal the great variety of natural beauty that has escaped the pressures of urban sprawl, the places where the ibis feeds in the salt marshes, where the beach plum covers the dunes with her spring blossoms, and the woodcock starts up from the cattails. These walks particularly call for you to bring along your binoculars and to proceed quietly along the paths.

Three of these walks are in very close proximity to "civilization," one being noisily close to Kennedy International Airport and the others only a few hundred feet from solid residential areas. That said, you'll find it easy to ignore the man-made noises and concentrate on the natural world. The birds and small animals are clearly undisturbed by their urban surroundings, and so can we be.

Another point to be made is that these walks may surprise you with the great numbers of waterfowl that now winter here, as compared to a few decades ago. Canada geese are especially common. At times it seems as though they have become permanent residents, not just visitors on their way south or north.

Shu Swamp Preserve

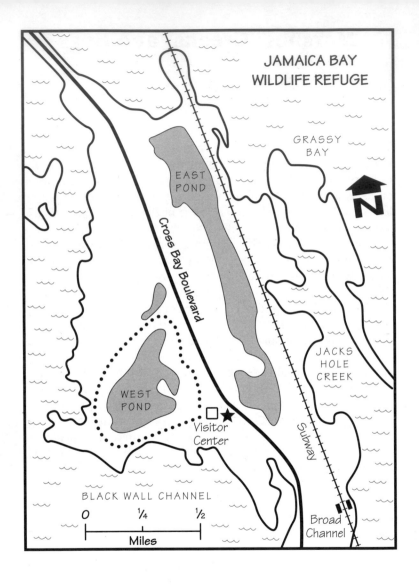

JAMAICA BAY
WILDLIFE REFUGE

GRASSY
BAY

EAST
POND

N

Cross Bay Boulevard

JACKS
HOLE
CREEK

WEST
POND

Subway

Visitor
Center

BLACK WALL CHANNEL

0   ¼   ½

Miles

Broad
Channel

36

Jamaica Bay Wildlife Refuge

The sun sets in a splash of color behind the towers of the city. A jumbo jet floats silently into Kennedy Airport on the other side of the bay. And West Pond at Jamaica Bay's Wildlife Refuge is alive, teeming with swooping terns, black skimmers seining their dinners through their amazing red bills, plovers and phalaropes skittering about in the shallows, the great egret and great blue heron standing majestic in the tall reeds. This is late afternoon in early August. The juxtaposition here of what man hath wrought in the distance with the magnificence of nature in the foreground calls attention to the question of whether we can keep a balance between these sometimes inimical forces.

You need a permit to visit the refuge, but one is available (free) at the front desk of the visitor center, which is open daily 8:30 A.M. to 5:00 P.M. The refuge is now a part of Gateway National Recreation Area and hence the national park system.

If you care to drive, take the Belt Parkway to exit 17S, then turn south onto Cross Bay Boulevard. There is a parking lot at the visitor center; look for the one discreet sign. Or you can come by subway. The IND Far Rockaway A train takes you there (Broad Channel stop). Walk west from the station 3 short blocks through a residential area to Cross Bay Boulevard, then turn right and proceed 0.75 mile to the refuge entrance.

The refuge itself is comprised of approximately 10,000 acres, much of it islands and tidal marshes. The accessible spot is the West Pond region, and West Pond is a forty-five-acre brackish pond with a fine 1.5-mile trail around it. A first trip to the Jamaica Bay Refuge is inspiring, especially undertaken at sunrise or sunset. Those responsible for seeing the possibilities, creating here a forever-wild area available to birds on the Atlantic Flyway and people via the subway, deserve highest praise and homage. Sit on one of the benches and turn your glasses or scope on these creatures. Many will use Jamaica Bay as a regular stopover during spring or fall migrations. Maybe as you sit here, the short-eared owl will rise from the grasses and swoop about on his nocturnal search for a mouse or two. Even if you don't know one bird from another, the whole setting will impress you.

There are a few suggestions we'd make for enhancing your enjoyment here. Bring along your bird book and binoculars and, if it's a buggy time of year, your favorite insect repellent. Although there's usually a breeze and the bugs may not bother you, in some grassy protected areas you may wish you had your repellent along. Also, eat before you come. There are several picnic tables available outside the visitor center—which is the *only* area for picnicking—and there is no place to dine nearby. Remember too, please, that this is a nature refuge, not a park, so conduct that would disturb the wildlife (jogging, radios, pets, cycling) is not permitted.

Across on the east side of the road, there is another, larger section of the refuge with a one-hundred-acre pond and shoreline on the bay as well. Sometimes rare birds stop here, and you may want to take a look, if you have strength after your walk around West Pond. If so, check first with the visitor center for trail conditions.

Please remember that all the vegetation makes a fine habitat for ticks and poison ivy, so take proper precautions against both.

The mailing address for information is Jamaica Bay Wildlife Refuge, Gateway NRA, Floyd Bennett Field, Brooklyn, NY 11234; (718) 318–4340.

37

John F. Kennedy Memorial Wildlife Sanctuary

As you fly into Kennedy Airport, you realize that the surrounding area is a vast network of tidal marshes, low-lying islands like lily pads in the bay, and barrier beaches conspicuously uninhabited by humans, which causes us to speculate on wildlife there. Knowing that the sea rising over a marsh floods this land with nutritive riches, that the ocean moderates temperatures here, and that wildlife in wetlands is abundant, we are intrigued by the thousands of acres behind Jones and Tobay Beaches. If you speculate about this as we do, then we must recommend to you the John F. Kennedy Memorial Wildlife Sanctuary.

It is a 500-acre stretch, swallowed up by more than 5,000 acres owned by Oyster Bay Town and managed by the New York State Environmental Conservation Department, but it provides an opportunity to investigate something of what wetlands life is about. You must obtain a permit to visit the sanctuary, either by mail (write to the Oyster Bay Department of Parks, Beach Division, 977 Hicksville Road, Massapequa, NY 11758 for an application) or by going to the office in person to get the permit on the spot. It is 1 block south of the Jerusalem Avenue intersection. Office hours are 9:00 A.M. to 4:30 P.M. daily; the telephone number is (516) 797–4114.

When you have your permit, get on the Ocean Parkway and

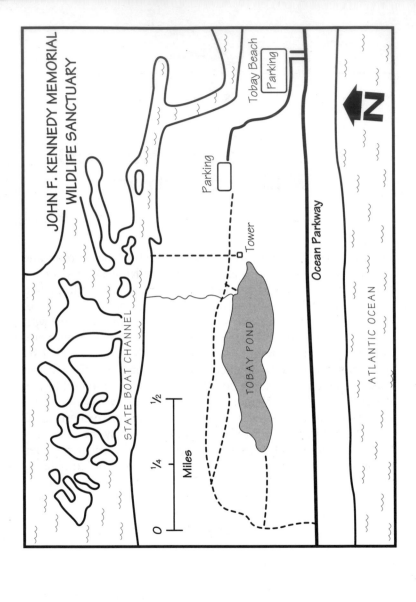

go east about 4 miles from the Jones Beach traffic circle to the Tobay Beach parking lot (just east of parking area 9). Drive west along the south border of the lot and along a road to the parking area provided for the sanctuary.

There is an old road, more than a mile long, that leads through the middle of the area and provides good footing, although it's absolutely flat and unspectacular because it is bordered by plants growing to a height just over your head. You can leave the road in several places and walk to blinds or to the observation tower from which you can sweep your glasses over the pond and the treetops, but you cannot get much closer to the water on foot.

It was after Labor Day when we walked here, spent a longer time and walked farther than we intended, and were exhausted. From the tower we had watched a large brown female marsh hawk for some time, quartering low over the marshes, her white rump patch distinctly visible, her buoyant, tilting glide a joy to observe. There were clouds of tree swallows swooping about, and low cherry trees alive with cedar waxwings. We thought we saw a prothonotary warbler. Glossy ibises flew purposefully overhead. Ducks arrived at the pond, skidding in for a landing. Kingbirds and white egrets were common, herons and belted kingfishers scarce.

The black-and-orange monarch butterflies were assembled in spectacular concentrations. These frail insects are noted for the long treks they make on their annual mass migrations and all morning continuously called attention to their flutterings.

Bayberry bushes were heavy with fruit; catbrier was in tangles. We noticed that birds had eaten the berries from the pokeweed. When we stretched out to rest on the white sandy dunes that overlook the pond from the northwest, we looked up at a sky everywhere interrupted by winged creatures.

38

Tackapausha Preserve

This surprising preserve encompasses eighty acres and a fine small museum in the middle of suburbia. A visit provides a pleasant contrast to the surrounding bustle and noise of this heavily developed area. The preserve is essentially a 1.5-mile-long and 1,000-foot-wide strip of woodland surrounding a freshwater stream (Seaford Creek) as it runs south toward the bay. It has three sections, separated by Clark Street and the Sunrise Highway (Route 27), with the southern one, where the museum stands, starting just north of Merrick Road on Washington Avenue. Trails run along each side of the brook, so you can easily get up to a 3.5-mile loop walk if desired. Also, for the ambitious, there is a blazed link between these trails and the trails of Massapequa Preserve (see Walk 39); it runs along the north side of the Sunrise Highway.

Because the stream meanders and branches, there are lots of marshy areas and little ponds along the way, and to the sides there are taller trees. In the southern part you'll see white oak, red maple, and one of the very few remaining stands of Atlantic white cedar on Long Island. There are shadbush, spicebush, and highbush blueberry. On the ground you'll see ferns and, in spring, flowers such as wood anemones and pink lady's slippers.

Because of the variety of plants and insects, there are many different birds at any time of the year. A pamphlet listing nearly

200 species and times of year when you might expect to see them is available at the museum.

The central section is comprised of fifteen acres and a pond where mallards, green herons, and other waterbirds can be found. The northern section, forty-five acres, is mostly a maple and oak forest, since it is higher and better drained, with wildflowers common in the open areas.

The museum building is a division of the Nassau County Museum of Natural History and well worth a visit. Inside there are informative displays, literature, and usually a nature film to see. Behind it there's a small menagerie with Long Island wildlife, allowing you a good close look at a red-tailed hawk, for instance. The museum is open Tuesday through Saturday 10:00 A.M. to 4:00 P.M., and Sunday 1:00 to 4:00 P.M., with a $2.00 admission fee for adults. The preserve, however, is open dawn to dusk. If you have questions, call (516) 571–7443.

The name Tackapausha, incidentally, is preserved on the original deed for the land in Hempstead. Tackapausha was one of the sachems who agreed to the transfer of land to the early settlers. And that's all we know about him.

39

Massapequa Preserve

Like the Tackapausha Preserve (see Walk 38), this has three sections: southern (Merrick Road to the Sunrise Highway), central (to Clark Boulevard), and northern (to Linden Street). Massapequa Preserve is 423 undeveloped acres of woodlands, ponds, lakes, and freshwater wetlands that border Massapequa Creek. The preserve is managed by the Nassau County Department of Recreation and is the largest passive-use park in the county. It is a quiet place in the midst of superhighways and dense population that offers a pleasant walk of a couple of miles up and back. A crystal-clear stream flowed freshly when we walked here; some kids fished at one of the dams, and two boys had a little rubber raft in the stream. The Massapequa Preserve is a wooded strip, drained by a stream dammed in a couple of places, thus making rather weedy ponds, excellent cover for ducks. The walking is either along a paved bicycle path that runs by the stream or along the Greenbelt-blazed foot trail, although there are paths into the woods and around ponds. In August the fragrance of sweet pepperbush permeated the air. We watched a least tern hover and dip over a pond, slamming into the water to capture a tiny minnow, and a family of black ducks float secretively through the reeds. Deep rose petals of the rose mallow flower, with their bright yellow centers, made a handsome display along the edge of the stream.

For an extended walk, park by Massapequa Lake at Merrick Road and follow the white-blazed Nassau-Suffolk Greenbelt Trail from its beginning there north to the Sunrise Highway and on to Clark Boulevard. From there on in the northern part you'll have paved bicycle path on the east most of the way up to Linden Street. Parking is possible almost anywhere on Parkside Boulevard or Lake Shore Drive.

If you're really ambitious, you can follow the Greenbelt up to Bethpage State Park (about 6 miles) or all the way to Stillwell Woods and Cold Spring Harbor on the North Shore. The whole 22-mile stretch is best taken in easy stages!

In summer and in migration times, Massapequa Lake will usually have ospreys in evidence, and in winter a great variety of ducks (canvasback, coot, ruddy, and more) will be at home. Other areas along the stream will reward you with whorled pogonia, white-fringed orchis, sundew, and more. The whole complex provides scarce habitat for many species and green space for people, making ecologists and nature enthusiasts rejoice. Similar areas can be found all along this south side of the glacial outwash plain.

Like Tackapausha, Massapequa Preserve is normally open dawn to dusk.

40

Charles T. Church Nature Sanctuary (Shu Swamp)

The Charles T. Church Nature Sanctuary is the jewel of the several properties owned and managed in the Mill Neck/Locust Valley area by the North Shore Wildlife Sanctuary, Inc. Tracing its origins back to 1929, this small but beautiful Shu Swamp preserve features both wetlands and uplands, with most of the wildlife drawn there by the clear waters of Beaver Brook fed by many springs and seeps. The burbling water talks to you, as do the voices of the birds. *Shu* is an old Dutch word that means "cascading waters." It's a lovely place to walk, passing on both sides of the marshy estuary that is a habitat for nesting great horned owls and wood ducks, mink, muskrats, and Trout. It's also home to evanescent spring flowers such as the trout lily, marsh marigold, dwarf ginseng and a rare shrub called hearts-a-Bustin, found nowhere else in New York State.

One thing we must stress—wildlife preserves are not recreation areas, so that while visitors are welcome during daylight hours all year, they are asked to observe the posted rules, which forbid fires, camping, picnics, dogs, or any conduct not in keeping with the purposes for which these sanctuaries were established.

The sanctuary is open daily, except Friday, between 7:00 A.M. and 7:00 P.M. April through October, and 7:00 A.M. to 5:00 P.M. November through March. Note that the parking area is locked after hours, and parking along the road guarantees a ticket. A full-time warden, Mr. Thomas Hornosky, is in charge. The address is P.O. Box 214, Mill Neck, NY 11765; (516) 671–0283. To reach the parking area, turn north off Route 25A onto Wolver Hollow Road and follow it until it ends at Chicken Valley Road. Go right and continue 1.6 miles to Frost Mill Road. It leads right, bends left, and continues north to a viaduct over which the Long Island Rail Road tracks cross. The sanctuary parking area is just south of the tracks and west of Frost Mill Road.

We are prompted to write a few words about the tulip tree, because the magnificent stand of tulip trees here along estuarial waters is inspiring, towering as they do probably 100 feet high, their trunks tall and straight and branchless for the first 50 or 60 feet. Considered the handsomest eastern forest tree because of its upright trunk and perfect symmetry, the tulip tree is frequently seen as an ornamental and is scattered throughout Long Island. However, the stand here is rare, perhaps unique, in its number of trees well over 150 years old. Their old bark is rich brown and deeply fissured, and some must have diameters of 4 feet or more. Another name by which this tree is known is canoe tree, because the Native Americans made their dugouts from them; when the English settlers first arrived, they found the Natives traveling all about Long Island in them. Surrounded by these ancient trees, looking up at those towering trunks, you may see how this was possible—though without modern tools it took great ingenuity and patience, skill with fire, and endless hours to fashion a seagoing craft of one. These trees give you reason to gasp and to consider the wonder of it all.

The North Shore Wildlife Sanctuary, Inc., is, like The Nature Conservancy, a private organization grateful for your donations.

41

South Shore Nature Center

The South Shore Nature Center in East Islip is an interesting place to visit, for its 206 acres of woods and marsh give it a character rather different from most other South Shore preserves. In the first place, it is special because of the range of habitats it offers to wildlife—from a sandy shoreline on Great South Bay to marshes and then a dry upland forest. Second, it has been so untouched by humans that the 1.75 miles of trails are defined solely by dense underbrush in the woods and by plank walks in the wetter areas; no blazes are needed. Indeed, the woods can be so dense that you can hear countless varieties of birds without seeing them.

The preserve is jointly owned by the town of Islip, Suffolk County, and The Nature Conservancy, having been established in 1977 as a public recreation and outdoor education facility. The town of Islip manages the area. All of the properties that make up the center were left in a natural state by their various owners well back into the previous century. As a consequence, there is great variety in the fauna and flora.

Most of the preserve's trees are red maple and black tupelo, which are found growing along the course of a stream and beside the boardwalks that span the preserve. An understory of sweet pepperbush, swamp azalea, and skunk cabbage flourishes in the freshwater bottomland along the stream, which flows through a

small pond. Black cherry, white and black oak, mockernut hickory, and sassafras compete with the maple and tupelo in the preserve's drier northeastern part.

A large variety of woodland and aquatic birds visits the preserve in all seasons. Shorebirds such as sandpipers have also been seen in the freshwater areas as well as in the brackish region near salt water. Deer, small mammals, reptiles, and amphibians are also present—as are mosquitoes, since so much of the surface water barely moves through the marshy areas.

The trail system is most easily followed by taking the Upland Trail west and south from its start, close to the nature center museum building. The first 0.25 mile goes through terrain that is high enough to be above standing groundwater, and as a result has a heavy growth of oak, mockernut hickory, and pitch pine. There are two side loops to the trail in this area that offer other glimpses of undisturbed habitat.

The first major trail junction on your left is marked to take you back to the nature center; the one on your right is now the Freshwater Trail. Follow it and in a few minutes you'll come to another junction, with the Saltwater Trail on your right, leading down through marshy terrain toward Great South Bay. The left fork is the other route back.

The Saltwater Trail threads its way on elevated walkways through swamp and marshy areas overloaded with tall phragmites reeds, past a good-sized pond on your right, and down to a final junction. The left branch is your route back to the nature center, and the right one takes you a short distance to a viewing platform close to a large saltwater pond that directly connects with Great South Bay.

The preserve serves the local population well, not just by the museum and trails, but also through naturalists who are steadily engaged in teaching school and other groups about the trees and animals that make for a balanced ecological mix. There is a picnic area, an indoor honeybee hive, and a butterfly garden; the nature museum has a salt water fish tank and reptiles. It is open daily from 9:00 A.M. to 5:00 P.M April through October (free admission). It is open weekdays only in late fall and winter. For more information, you can call (631) 224–5436 or stop in the museum for informative pamphlets and a trail guide booklet.

To reach the preserve, take Route 111 south from any of the major arteries (Long Island Expressway–Route 495, exit 56; Southern State Parkway, exit 43; Sunrise Highway–Route 27, Islip Avenue exit) to the end of Route 111 at the Montauk Highway (Route 27A). Go left (east) on it about 0.8 mile to Bayview Avenue. Turn right onto Bayview; the preserve entrance will be on your right in about 0.8 mile.

42

Peconic River

South of Middle Country Road (Route 25) and west of Calverton is a large, sparsely populated area, mostly woodlands, with a series of ponds that form the stream that meanders to Riverhead, making the Peconic River the longest on Long Island. It is Robert Cushman Murphy County Park, a long, narrow strip of land on which Horn, Round, Peasys, Woodchoppers, Duck, Sandy, Grassy, Twin, and Jones Ponds follow one after another north to south. There are many sandy woods roads in this undeveloped area that make for pleasant walking—so many of them, in fact, that you need to pay close attention to your route so you don't get disoriented. The best map available is the one featuring the Long Island Pine Barrens Trail—West Section. (See the comments on this subject in Walk 23.) You can go safely any time of year, except during the winter hunting season. Call the New York State Department of Environmental Conservation at (631) 444–0310 for the exact dates of the open season, and to get the required permit.

This area supports considerable wildlife. Deer are plentiful, and bird life abounds. We have seen at least twenty different mushroom species over the years. (Although we have rushed home afterward to look in our mushroom guide, we have never done more than photograph them.) The great blue heron lives in Woodchoppers Pond. You will see several species of ducks, little green herons, a Canada goose family, and, in spring, warblers,

PECONIC RIVER

2 miles west on Rt. 25
Pine Trail Preserve Parking Lot

Middle Country Road

Robert Cushman
Murphy
County Park

Wading

Grumman Blvd.

HORN
POND

ROUND
POND

PEASYS
POND

River Manorville Road

N

WOODCHOPPERS
POND

DUCK
POND

SANDY
POND

GRASSY
POND

Schultz Road

½

¼

TWIN
PONDS

Y=Brookhaven Trail

W=Pine Barrens Trail
(Paumanok Path)

JONE'S
POND

0

W

Miles

KENTS
POND

orioles, scarlet tanagers, partridges, and woodcocks. In summer kingbirds are often seen. We were thrilled to see the rare red crossbill among the pitch pine and oak. The shores of the ponds are marshy, and in fall the colors are riotous. During rainy periods the trail can be wet in spots.

The half day or more you spend in this area will be peaceful—maybe an angler will be here, but we have met only one other hiker in the woods though we have walked here many times.

A good access to these boggy ponds is an unmarked road 2.3 miles north of the Long Island Expressway exit 69 on Wading River/Schultz Road or 1.2 miles south on Wading River/Schultz Road from Route 25 and just opposite Wading River–Manorville Road. It is a gated dirt road, with only informal provisions for parking on either side, near the posted signs reading COOPERATIVE HUNTING AREA. Another dirt road entry is on Middle Country Road, directly opposite a paved road named Panamoka Trail. Suffolk County Park's Pine Trail Preserve parking lot affords a way to visit this area. It is a couple of hiking miles to the west, on the south side of Middle County Road, 0.5 mile east of William Floyd Parkway. Another path running through this park is the Brookhaven Trail. It runs north from the Paumanok Path through a wild and beautiful section of the pine barrens.

43

Cranberry Bog

A rather large area of county-owned land right in Riverhead is a 211-acre former cranberry bog. It is a unique haven for plant and animal life, probably the only habitat of this type remaining on Long Island. Although it is unmarked, it is a favorite haunt of naturalists and has an interesting history.

In the early 1800s the Peconic River was in demand as a source of waterpower for mill wheels, but after the Civil War coal and other fuels took over, and the water was no longer needed as much. Someone had the sensible idea of using these lowlands and the abundant water for raising cranberries, and the resulting industry flourished from about 1875 to the 1930s, at one point becoming the third largest producer of cranberries in the country. These small bogs could not compete with the major growers elsewhere, however; operating costs rose, and in 1959 a major pesticide used on cranberries gave the death blow by turning out to be carcinogenic.

This area is now held by Suffolk County as a preserve and nature-oriented park for its residents. An environmental staff oversees the preserve, but it is open for nature walks on an informal basis.

To find it, drive south on Route 63, which leads from Riverhead Circle toward Wildwood Lake. Just south of the Lakeside Drive intersection, you will find a large yellow SUFFOLK COUNTY

PARKS sign marking a recessed parking area.

The gate at the front of the park is intended to discourage motorized traffic. You can easily walk around it to the unmarked trails. The place makes a fascinating ramble. A bridge over the Little River makes it possible to make a loop around Sweezy Pond. The old cranberry fields lie to the east of the pond, and dikes permit you to penetrate some of the jungly growth. We say it is a ramble because to enjoy this spot is to explore, walking here and there along fringes of the wetlands. But we implore you: Walk quietly and cautiously, respecting stillness and wildlife. Deer and herons, swans and geese as well as ducks, live here, so try especially hard not to disturb. This is one of the few places left on Long Island where you can find a stand of Atlantic white cedar. The variety of shrubs and ground cover is also extraordinary—sweet pepperbush, bayberry, beach plum, wild grape, bearberry, cranberry, bear oak, many bog plants—and the pond is full of water lilies, slender arrowheads, and reeds, a catalog of freshwater swamplands growth. If you like this kind of exploring, you should enjoy a leisurely stroll here.

Incidentally, there is another series of old cranberry bogs nearby that is worth visiting. Referring to the Walk 42 map, take Wading River–Manorville Road southeast from its junction with Schultz Road 1.1 miles to Old River Road (left). Proceed for about 1 mile on Old River Road to its junction with River Road. The bogs run both north and south from this point along a small stream that drains Swan Pond into the Peconic River. It's a pleasant area, often frequented by deer that come to drink from the stream.

Quogue Wildlife Refuge

The New York State Department of Environmental Conservation has had, since 1952, a long-term lease to manage this refuge, a 300-acre parcel that is the headwaters and drainage basin of Quantuck Creek. This provides varied wetlands—swamp, freshwater bog, potholes, and ponds as well as tidal estuary. Also, there are dwarf pine barrens up at the north end. Altogether there are 8 miles of trails, with the main ones noted on the map. The details of the way the place has been developed suggest talented and dedicated professional guidance. The sanctuary lies just north of the railroad tracks above the village of Quogue on Old Country Road, which runs north of the Montauk Highway and makes its way around into Quogue-Riverhead Road (Route 104). Guided nature walks are available to groups and clubs for a modest fee. All groups should call the refuge for reservations. Educational programs are offered throughout the year. For more information call (631) 653–4771. Most of the trails are basically wheelchair accessible and appropriate for people of all ages and abilities. Rest rooms are open spring through autumn. South of the railroad tracks is the Fairy Dell estuarine tract. This area is traversed by a 0.25-mile boardwalk that accommodates wheelchairs.

As you come into the preserve, there is a pen complex where animals are kept; most have been injured and are unable to re-

turn to the wild. On our visit there was a bald eagle, a bobcat, several wild turkeys, and other types of local animals. Ducks, geese, and other seasonal waterfowl roam at will at the pond's edge and use the adjacent area for foraging.

In spring Canada geese families go about training their young, parading in the grass, one parent ahead and one behind, with the little flock in between. Somehow they find the living so good here they stay year-round.

Walking is clear-cut. You can take the 0.7-mile path that goes around the main pond or the one that follows the perimeter of the refuge for more than 2 miles. We often decide to do both; a trail guide is available at the entrance booth.

Wherever you go you will see typical flora of the Long Island pine barrens—oak and pine interspersed with various berry bushes the birds like to feed on. The ground cover is bearberry and blueberry, black cherry, beach plum, and shadbush, as well as nearly seventy varieties of wildflowers that grow here. One summer we were delighted to find in a boggy spot a small stand of the exquisite, tiny, white-blossomed bog orchid; you may also find the insect-eating sundew and pitcher plants.

There are a number of places to sit and quietly observe, whichever path you take. Very often, on the ice pond on the north, there'll be a little green heron or some mallards. You can explore this refuge with no fear of getting lost. It is open daily from 9:00 A.M. to 5:00 P.M.

Sand Spits and Points

We've separated these walks from the sections devoted to Long Island's long, sandy shorelines, both north and south, mostly as a matter of convenience. These geographic features have the same water boundaries as the beaches and share the same varieties of vegetation and wildlife. Still, they are different in outlook, for most face land not very far off, most have calmer waters, and they just seem to have a different atmosphere.

One walk (Elizabeth A. Morton National Wildlife Refuge) is really practical only in fall and winter, as ospreys, piping plovers, and colonies of terns nest there April through August. The nesting areas are normally fenced off at that time to prevent people from disturbing these endangered birds.

The walks we've listed here all permit fairly extensive walking along the shoreline, though not as much as the beach walks. They remind us, though, that there are literally dozens of places where we can gain access to a calm shoreline, like these, in the off seasons. These are the town and county beaches that provide recreation along Great South Bay, the North Shore harbors, and the beaches along Peconic and Gardiners Bays. Other points of access are public roads that run right down to the water's edge. Usually there are parking restrictions, but off season and with local inquiry, you should be able to find many such places to walk.

Montauk Point, of course, is the one place that is fully exposed to the open Atlantic, and while it is often tranquil there, the steady erosion that is threatening the lighthouse tells of violent wave action at almost any time of the year. Also, in contrast to the other spots, Montauk has a quite extensive trail network inland from the beach that is worth exploring.

ELIZABETH A. MORTON
NATIONAL
WILDLIFE REFUGE

JESSUP'S NECK

NOYACK
BAY

LITTLE PECONIC
BAY

N

NOYACK CREEK

Clam
Island

Sag Harbor
3 miles

38

Noyac Road

1

½

0
Miles

45

Elizabeth A. Morton National Wildlife Refuge

Dividing Little Peconic Bay and Noyack Bay, jutting out from the north shore of the south fork of Long Island, just above Water mill, is Jessup's Neck. Of the numerous points, necks, and promontories that extend into the waters surrounding Long Island, this offers a wide variety of terrains, and walking here is great for many reasons. It is the Elizabeth Alexandra Morton National Wildlife Refuge and is managed by the U.S. Fish and Wildlife Service as a resting and feeding area for migratory birds. The refuge is open from sunrise till sunset.

Since the refuge offers a combination of beach, woods, ponds, and wetlands, walking is the ideal way for almost anyone to enjoy it, in any season and on any day. Entirely apart from the birding, the views over the waters are reason enough to visit.

The refuge is most easily reached by leaving the Montauk Highway (Route 27) on Deerfield Road about 0.4 mile east of Water Mill, and heading north on it until you reach Noyac Road. Turn right, and in about 0.5 mile you'll reach the refuge. Drive into the grounds through a gate on the northern side of Noyac Road; park here near an old barn a few hundred yards beyond. Stop at the kiosk, which has a map and pictures, for a leaflet about the refuge.

While there is an office in the little building to the right beyond the parking area, it is rarely staffed, so any questions should normally be addressed to the Long Island National Wildlife Refuge

Complex in Shirley (631–286–0485).

The path down to the bay is about 0.5 mile long and lined with many kinds of berry bushes—delectables for the land birds that frequent this quiet sanctuary. There is honeysuckle, myrtle, and rural charm. Be quiet and alert. We have come down this path on an early evening and surprised a graceful doe feasting on these same bushes. The path emerges upon a long, narrow strip of beach on the bay with a small inlet from Noyack Bay on your right. This area supports some 500 black ducks that winter here, as well as a variety of other waterbirds all year.

Now and then a clammer in the inlet leans out of his or her boat to scoop the bottom with a clamming rake. In fall or winter you'll see scallop boats dragging in the bay, though these juicy morsels are dwindling alarmingly, and nowhere else in the world does such a tiny, sweet, tender scallop exist.

The neck beyond this point is closed April 1 to September 1, so as to leave the ospreys, piping plovers, and least terns that nest here quite undisturbed while they are raising their young. There is one active osprey nest near the far end of the inlet lagoon that you can easily see even in the closed season. As for the rest of the peninsula, plan on visiting it in fall and winter only. When you can walk there, in about 1.5 miles you will come to a sharp rise and spread of land on a wooded promontory. We like to walk in the woods on the path and then return by the beach. At the beginning of the wooded path, there was once a farmhouse. In spring a carpet of daffodils appears out of the myrtle, splendid in color in this secluded habitat.

In the spring woods, during the warbler migration, you see some fifteen different varieties flitting among the big oaks before the leaves come out. And down on the beach to the west of the neck, look out to the fish weir. Ospreys and cormorants often sit on poles where the pickings are concentrated.

As you walk along the trails, the chickadees will rustle in the brush and chirp to you. If you hold sunflower seeds out in your open palms and are still and patient, they will land on your fingers and eat out of your hands.

The Morton Refuge can be a cool and refreshing place in summer, when the afternoon breeze from the southwest whistles across the neck. In winter, when the bay freezes solid, if the winds across the ice are too chilling, there are many protected areas of woodland to the east before you reach the bay, and calm shelter for a walk under cover. One early spring we discovered a strangely eerie sight: dry white bones in a bed of greenest myrtle, the carcass of a deer dead of starvation or exhaustion. Later the refuge manager told us he had taken the skeleton to a school for preservation.

When you leave the parking area, you will quickly see a path leading right. This is a loop trail about 0.4 mile long that winds past a pond and through woods (devastated by Hurricane Bob in 1991) to rejoin the main trail about halfway to the beach.

Incidentally, this is one of more than 500 refuges managed by the U.S. Fish and Wildlife Service throughout the United States—many of them provide similar opportunities for walking and observing wildlife.

As with all other government parks, monuments, and refuges, there is a standard daily parking fee of $4.00 per private car or motorbike. Annual passes are also available for $12.00 for any one refuge, as well as several "Golden" passes for seniors or the disabled. For specifics, call the Fish and Wildlife Service at (631) 286–0485.

On your way to the Elizabeth A. Morton National Wildlife Refuge, you will pass Laurel Valley, a Suffolk County park off Deerfield Road, just south of Noyac Road. Parking is on the shoulder on the east side of the road, opposite the NORTH SIDE HILLS sign. Look for a kiosk. The trails in this enchantingly beautiful little park were cut, and blazed by the Southhampton Trails Preservation Society, which continues to maintain them. Someday soon the Paumanok Path will connect with a trail that transects this 148-acre parcel of land. The rolling knoll-and-kettle topography, beech, dense laurel, farmland being reclaimed by cedar, foxes, and red-tailed hawks all make this a lovely place to visit. For information and maps, you can contact the preservation society at (631) 537–5202.

46

Cedar Point County Park

In the town of East Hampton, 6.5 miles directly north of Georgica, occupying one of the many peninsulas that jut into Gardiners Bay and give this area such meandering shapes, is Cedar Point, a choice park of 600 acres. This is a Suffolk County park, and you will find parking space here, as in all Suffolk County parks, limited to Suffolk County residents with permits. Trails are not heavy-traffic areas, and hikers are not discouraged. For information call (631) 852–7620.

To find the park entrance if you're headed east on the Montauk Highway (Route 27), slow down as you pass the East Hampton Airport. The road signs were not made to be read while traveling 40 miles per hour. Turn north onto the first road past the airport, Stephen Hands Path. Continue on it 2 miles, across Route 114; it connects with Old Northwest Road, which bears off to your left. Continue on this for 1.8 miles to a fork, where you turn right onto Northwest Road, and drive 1.7 miles to the crossing with Alewive Brook Road. Jog left and enter the park there to the north. Or, if you're driving from East Hampton, follow Three Mile Harbor Road and turn left on Springy Banks Road, which also runs into Alewive Brook Road.

You enter the Northwest Woods, a high bluff generally 50 feet above the waters of Gardiners Bay to the north, and drop down alongside Alewive Pond to Cedar Pond, near which you'll find a camping and parking area. There are deer in these woods; look sharply in the late afternoon. When you park, you can walk out on the spit, which points west. It's a fine walk, with a striking granite lighthouse at the tip. And though surely you may temporarily lose your sense of direction, you'll look south onto Northwest Harbor and Barcelona Point, northwest onto Shelter Island, north onto Orient Beach State Park, and east onto Gardiners Island; eventually the geography of these fingers and watery shores will sort itself out.

There's a good nature trail (leaflets available) running from the park office area opposite Alewive Pond, 0.7 mile out to an observation platform at the top of the bluffs overlooking Gardiners Bay. On a clear day you should easily see the Connecticut shore 15 miles away beyond Orient Point.

The walk west to Cedar Point is just over a mile. The inner shore is sandy, the outer one pebbly. From this entry east along a stretch of wild beaches to Lafarges Landing is a distance of 2 miles. Jingle shells, scallop shells, boat shells, or slipper shells and pear-shaped whelks are nature's handiworks you'll find here, along with all the other flotsam that gives beachcombing variety. Between the open woods and the sand spit, there is a lot of fine habitat for birds.

The park is open all year, basically from 8:00 A.M. to dusk. That means the gates close about 4:00 P.M. November through February. In 1985, after a public referendum enabled East Hampton to purchase 516 acres of the Grace Estate, a lovely hiking area was opened up to the public. The town's purchase protected a vital part of the Northwest Woods, including harbor, shoreline, and freshwater ponds. Lee Dion, a prominent member of the East Hampton Trails Preservation Society, created East Hampton's Own Ghost Town a 3-mile self-guided tour through an abandoned Northwest settlement. It is a captivating walk through history that starts from a parking area 0.2 mile west of Alewive Brook Road on Northwest Road. Your experience of this area will be greatly enriched if you mail a self-addressed stamped envelope to EHTPS, P.O. Box 2144, Amagansett, NY 11930 and ask for the free Ghost Town Tour.

47

Orient Beach State Park

At the end of Route 25 on the north fork of Long Island, just before you get to the water and the ferry to New London, on your right is the usual rustic state park sign for Orient Beach—but Orient Beach is not a usual state park. Turn and drive along the causeway to the parking lot. If it's spring or early summer, look to your right as you go along the causeway for the osprey nest across the water. A faithful pair returns yearly, and they are magnificent birds, these fish hawks. Sometimes you can watch them fish, diving from on high and catching a fish as much as 10 feet below the surface with their talons.

The park (631–323–2440 or 631–669–1000) is open daily all year, 8:00 A.M. to 4:30 P.M. October through May, 8:00 A.M. to 6:00 P.M. in June and September, and 8:00 A.M. to 8:00 P.M. in July and August. Ask about the guided and self-guided nature trails. and the bike trail. The parking fee is $7.00 in June, July, and August. After 4:00 P.M. there is never a charge. The summer months are the most crowded time and not one we particularly recommend, because when you walk from the parking lot out onto the beach and turn to your right, you'll find it is a favorite picnicking and swimming spot with food service and a bathhouse nearby. One hundred yards past the lifeguard, however, you escape the bulk of the crowd. As you move around the curve of the beach, you have the choice of keeping to the edge of the water or following the jeep tracks into the interior of this spit. You may be confused because

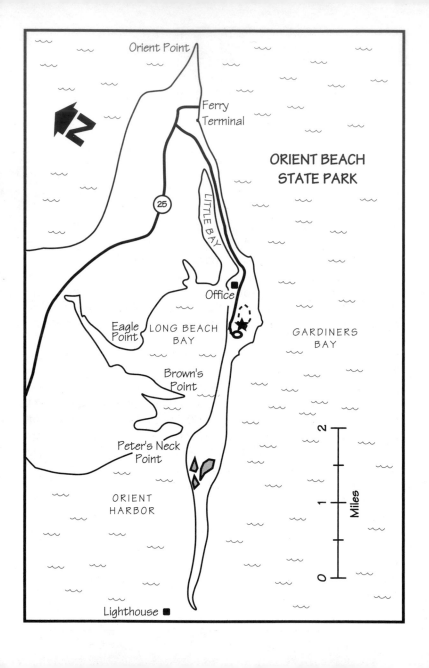

Orient Point

Ferry
Terminal

**ORIENT BEACH
STATE PARK**

25

LITTLE BAY

Office

Eagle
Point

LONG BEACH
BAY

GARDINERS
BAY

Brown's
Point

Peter's Neck
Point

ORIENT
HARBOR

2

Miles

1

0

Lighthouse ■

Orient Point looks to the northeast, but this narrow strip of land that is Orient Beach, 4 miles long, runs to the southwest.

What makes it unusual? It affords beautiful views of Gardiners Bay and its shores and islands. Wander at will among the scrub pines, for you are never far from salt water on either side. There are two ponds in the interior that attract waterbirds, and here among the stunted pines and wetlands there is a herd of deer that comes and goes to the mainland. Although we have seen their tracks many times, we have actually seen the deer only fleetingly in winter. You cannot be quiet enough to surprise these wily, graceful creatures, but how they can conceal themselves in this narrow quarter is a mystery. They blend in and get lost as nature intended.

A good plan is to go out by the beach, pebbly but not bad footing, and back through the interior. Wilderness areas are ideal for shell collecting and bird-watching; be certain to bring along binoculars. If you get as far as the tip, you will come near the handsomely rebuilt Long Beach Bar Light (locally called the "Bug" Light), whose predecessors guided fishing boats into Greenport. Be prepared, though, to find this farthest end closed to visitors in spring and summer, since then it is home to a nesting colony of piping plovers.

Incidentally, now that you've come this far east, you ought to continue a couple of blocks farther north to the parking area at the absolute end of Route 25, just beyond the New London ferry terminal. If you leave your car there and walk along the beach about 0.5 mile to the bitter end, you'll enjoy a panorama of Long Island Sound and the Connecticut shore, Block Island Sound, Montauk Point, Gardiners Island, and Gardiners Bay. Directly across the tide rips of Plum Gut is Plum Island, a closed area that is home to the U.S. Department of Agriculture's Animal Disease Center.

You should also make the time to walk the new Latham Maritime Forest Trail, a nice nature trail that starts out at the north end of the parking lot, then meanders up the spit and down again to the parking area. It's well laid out and has a very relevant leaflet for the dozen stations along it.

48

Montauk Point Parks

This is an extremely popular area, and the crowds may put you off, but don't let them—you'd be missing too much if you did. Choose your time and move away from crowds. Montauk is an experience, and you are apt to enjoy it if you are a loner and nature lover. There's a raw bleakness here: hills of shadbush and bayberry, almost endless dunes, and an incessant surf chewing away at the boulders, tumbling stones that cackle in a noisy babble. We've come here at dawn before the sun was up at least twice and will come again. If you come at this hour, you won't be alone. Surf fishers will be here before you. You can walk for miles in either direction. We've been here at midday and at sunset, too, lingering afterward in the twilight. So although it is wiser to rhapsodize about winter, spring, or fall, our experience is that there's something for you in any season at any hour of day in Montauk.

The public lands east of Lake Montauk are quite extensive; they include the 724-acre state park that extends west from the point about 2 miles to encompass the northern shoreline and Oyster Pond. Directly west of it is Suffolk County's Theodore Roosevelt County Park, whose 1,200 acres cover Shagwong Point and most of the remaining land east of East Lake Drive (excluding a residential area at the middle section of that road). The next property is the undeveloped 700-acre Camp Hero State

Park. It is located south of the highway and away from the lighthouse and was formerly the site of an air force radar station. Although it is not easily accessible, the bluffs are impressive when viewed from the beach. Finally, west of Camp Hero is a new 330-acre nature sanctuary.

The present county park headquarters building, called the Third House, dates in part to 1806, when it was erected for those tending cattle on the surrounding 10,000-acre common pasture. Since then it has served as a residence for Theodore Roosevelt and his Rough Riders after the Spanish-American War, and in the 1930s it became the Deep Hollow Guest and Cattle Ranch. Today the only remaining horsey aspect is a riding stable. The hilly terrain here offers good protection from bad weather, and as a result many varieties of birds and animals inhabit the area.

Where to go at the point? Start by visiting the lighthouse and the fine small museum there that will give you a better understanding of the continuing conflict between sea and humanity here. Ocean storms erode the point and endanger the lighthouse; people move in boulders at the base of the bluffs to lessen erosion, and are attempting, successfully we're told, to cover the steep slope with vegetation that holds the soil in place.

Then follow the path north of the lighthouse down into the gully to the little pond. Wildflowers, birds of the thicket, and pond life are here. Then cross over the dunes onto the beach and walk south to the point. If you're here at low tide, you can walk as far south and west along the rocky shore as you are able. The other direction—northwest along the beach fronting Block Island Sound—is a less crowded walk; the farther you go, the fewer the people and the more abundant the shorebirds. Montauk is a prime birding area, especially for Arctic seabirds.

These parks cover a large area, so if you walk only those beaches easily accessible from the main parking area, you have not done justice to the region.

Traveling north of the parkway on East Lake Drive, you will cross over the Paumanok Path. This portion of the path runs along the parkway right-of-way, as it does east of Hither Hills.

Considering how close this trail is to a major road, you will be pleasantly surprised by the wild experience it offers you. If you continue north on East Lake Drive, after approximately 2 miles you will find parking for the Big Reed Pond trail system. Immediately after the SUFFOLK COUNTY PARKS sign, turn right onto a dirt road, which will take you directly to a parkng area with an information kiosk. Suffolk County Parks distributes an excellent interpretive map of these nature trails.

East of the Oyster Pond overlook parking area, on the south side of Route 27, is the Point Woods shoulder parking on Camp Hero Road. On the west side of the road is a short access path to the Point Woods Trail. The maritime forest that this trail visits has huge holly trees, vernal ponds, and a wide variety of plant and animal life.

A special treat during winter is the Seal Haulout Trail. This trail can be accessed from the Point Woods Trail. If you follow the white-rectangle Paumanok Path blazes to the north across Route 27, you will enter a park entrance. Here you have the option of continuing west along the path to Oyster Pond and then Third House, or following the round plastic blazes that mark the Seal Haulout Trail. On sunny days, during low tide, the seals will pull themselves up onto the rocks close to shore.

A map of the entire Montauk area with the various trails is available at the county park headquarters on Route 27. A somewhat dated but more complete map is available from the town of East Hampton; refer to Walk 27 for the address.

If you have questions, call (631) 668–5000 for the state park, and (631) 852–7878 for the Suffolk County park. Both are open daily from 8:00 A.M. to 5:00 P.M.

North Shore Beaches and Bluffs

While similar in extent to the marvelous strands of the South Shore, these beaches are quite different in character. They tend in general to be more pebbly, since the sea here is constantly eroding not a long sandbar, but the back side of a glacial moraine. As a result, the beaches have lots of stones, from golf ball size up to impressive glacial erratics, so sandy spots for swimming and sunning are somewhat scarce. The stones, in turn, have been mined from a nearly continuous line of bluffs that mark the coast. These can be well over 100 feet high, as at Mount Sinai, and they are usually wooded up to the edge except where homes have been built. Both these factors often make beach access difficult even while providing fine views out over Long Island Sound. In many places the bluffs are so high and steep that the only way homeowners can get down to the water's edge is by erecting long wooden stairways down the face. The bluffs look most impressive when seen from a boat offshore; they must be intimidating close up!

There are a few places in the long stretch east of Port Jefferson where the bluffs are minimal. Most of these spots have either a public or private road down to the beach, for swimmers in summer and surf fishers at any time. In general we've usually encountered fewer people on these North Shore beaches than in the south. The parking situation noted for the Atlantic beaches, however, can also apply here.

One other factor that sets these shores apart is the tidal range. On the South Shore the range is only about 3 feet, and between high and low tides the look of the sandy strand changes very little. On the North Shore the range varies from about 4 feet at Horton Point to more than 7 feet at Glen Cove. This makes for a markedly different seashore, due to the exposed rocky intertidal zone.

49

Sunken Meadow
State Park

Sunken Meadow State Park is a grand place for walking, most particularly when it's not swimming weather. Choose a nice, crisp fall weekend to go or a soft spring day or even a misty summer's day, for there are miles to explore. An interesting inlet lies to the east, a bridle path to the south; the beach itself stretches as far west as you could wish, and in the middle of it all is a fine 0.75-mile boardwalk.

This beautiful park, which has one of the best sand beaches on the North Shore, was opened to the public back in the 1920s when the legendary Robert Moses acquired an abandoned estate here. He saw its possibilities for a public recreation area on the sound directly north of the state park that bears his name on the South Shore (see Walk 1). Now there are four large parking lots, three golf courses, picnic areas and playgrounds, and refreshment stands. Sunken Meadow is a highly organized place, well adapted to lots of visitors, but it all quiets down in the off season.

The walk we enjoy the most follows the Greenbelt Trail east, from its beginning at the footbridge close to the southwest end of parking field 3, along the high bluffs to Old Dock Road. There you can drop down to beach level and return along the shore until you can cross over again to lot 3. This 2.5-mile loop gives you fine views of the Nissequogue inlet and estuary, salt meadows, and a long stretch of beach extending in both directions. If field 3 is closed, park in field 1 and walk east to the bridge.

As you might expect, the 200 acres of sandy bluffs, brackish creeks, salt marshes, and heavily wooded uplands offer excellent habitat for birds in all seasons. Eighty-four varieties are common in one season or another, and sixty more are occasionally seen here, so bring your binoculars.

Stop at the park office in the building between the west end of field 1 and the sound, and get a free checklist and guide covering the 121 varieties that have been observed more than once in five years. It also shows the seasonal abundance for all these types of birds.

The park is open 6:30 A.M. to sunset in the summer season. The toll is now $7.00, and it is levied weekdays from 7:00 A.M. to 4:00 P.M. and on weekends from 7:00 A.M. to 6:00 P.M. in summer. The toll is collected on weekends from 8:00 A.M. to 4:00 P.M. in May and September through Columbus Day; at all other times the park is free (including summer weekdays for seniors). Questions? Call (631) 269–4333.

The best roads to take to reach the park are major arteries such as the Long Island Expressway (Route 495), the Jericho Turnpike (Route 25), the Northern State Parkway, and Route 25A. All of them intersect with and give easy access to the sole entrance road, the Sunken Meadow Parkway.

50

Nissequogue Estuary

A blazed trail, the Long Island Greenbelt, winds across the full width of Long Island and has since 1978, going northward 32 miles from Great South Bay to Long Island Sound. This was made possible through the inspiration and initiative of the Long Island Greenbelt Trail Conference, combined with the cooperative effort of the towns of Islip and Smithtown, Suffolk County, and New York State. It is a noteworthy accomplishment.

Anyone may walk the trail, which has locked gates where it enters nature preserves, but you must have a permit to get the lock combinations (call 631–265–1054, Caleb Smith State Park). The conference prints a map of the Long Island Greenbelt that shows this part of the trail in much more detail than our map. It is obtainable for $4.00 ($3.00 for members) through the Long Island Greenbelt Trail Conference, Inc., 23 Deer Path Road, Central Islip, NY 11722; (631) 360–0753.

After leaving Blydenburgh County Park and Caleb Smith State Park, both of which have walks (34 and 21) that can conveniently be done from a central location, the Greenbelt Trail heads north toward its end at Sunken Meadow State Park (see Walk 49). This section is a linear one, with more road walking than is desirable, so we can't really recommend the first part of it.

Most of the last 4.5 miles, however, are so rewarding that we urge you to find a friend and spot cars at each end so you can cover it more easily. The trail basically follows the south shore of

NISSEQUOGUE ESTUARY

LONG ISLAND SOUND

trail submerged during high tide

Field 3

Sunken Meadow State Park

Sunken Meadow Parkway

KINGS PARK

Old Dock Road

St. Johnland Road

Kings Park State Hospital

Obadiah Smith House

HARRISON POND

Smithtown Resident Parking Only

SAN REMO

25A

Rose Street

Landing Road

Riviera Road

Smithtown Landing Golf Club Parking Lot

N

0 1 2 Miles

the Nissequogue River, sometimes close to the water, sometimes well above it on bluffs. Check the tide tables. The portion of trail south of Old Dock Road is occassionally submerged and impassable during extreme high tide.

To start at the south end of this lovely stretch, find the corner where Route 25A makes a right-angle turn in San Remo, about 1.7 miles north of the junction with Route 25 in Smithtown. At the corner go straight east onto Rose Street for about 0.4 mile until it ends at Landing Avenue. Turn left there, and in 0.2 mile turn right into the long downhill driveway of the Smithtown Landing Club Town Park. Go down to the end of the parking lot. Park there amid the golfers, and find the Greenbelt blazes. They are vertical white blazes about 2 inches by 4 inches painted on trees, rocks, and posts; they should be easy to pick up here. The trail heads north along the shoreline again, reaches Riviera Road, and continues on it along the curve of the river. When you reach St. Johnland Road, the trail goes right for a short distance. Directly across the street the parking area for the Harrison Pond Town Park is an alternate place to leave a car.

Just below the Obadiah Smith House, the trail leaves the road and cuts north across the marsh. Go in here at the double blaze. Remember that a single blaze means you're still on the right track; a double one signals a change in direction.

The path crosses through tall reeds, follows along the river, climbs a bluff for a fine view, and continues on to Old Dock Road. You'll find a restaurant and boating facilities and another place you can park off season.

When you take the trail up the 150-foot bluff to the west, you enter Sunken Meadow State Park and can now follow the route along the top until you come down into the developed part of the park. There the trail makes a sharp turn across a footbridge to end just across the road from field 3, the northern end of the Greenbelt Trail. During winter field 3 may be closed, so you might have to park in field 4 or the east end of field 1.

From this last stretch of bluffs, you can see where the river reaches the sound; beyond it is Short Beach, which belongs to the village of Nissequogue, and Crane Neck Point across Smith-town Bay. Across the sound is Connecticut, of course, and the city with the tall buildings is Bridgeport. There are always boats of many sizes, which move in a businesslike way across the sound's waters and, in the river, swans, which have a close affinity to Long Island. This section of the trail provides picture-postcard views all along the bluffs, and when the waterfowl migrate, it can be spectacular. The bluffs are popular, so for the quiet moods that the trail does have, it is best to walk here early in the morning—or late on a summer's day to watch the sunset.

51

Wildwood State Park

Wildwood State Park is well out on the island, 73 miles east of New York City. It is roughly rectangular and has a frontage of about 1.5 miles on Long Island Sound. Situated on high ground with high bluffs, it covers just over 700 acres. There is good walking along the pebbly North Shore beach here. Also, within the park there are about 10 miles of trails through cleared woodland areas, offering easy-walking straightaways that are fairly level, nothing strenuous. It is a place that is open, protected, quiet, and wooded. And you can walk at a good clip.

Many of the North Shore beaches are private, not allowing easy access without trespassing, but there is a large parking lot here with a broad walkway leading down a gradual slope, less than 0.25 mile to the beach. The sand doesn't shift along these North Shore beaches as rapidly as it does along the Atlantic. The water freezes up much more quickly and warms earlier in spring. The ground is gravelly, and there are quite a few boulders, debris of the glacial period. Protected as the beach is by these high bluffs, it is a marked contrast to the ocean shore and offers good variety to a beach walker. There's less severe buffeting in windy weather, too. Those close relatives of the crab—barnacles—have attached themselves to all boulders. Seaweed in many forms is exposed. Periwinkles and whelks abound. The narrow strip of this tidal zone teems with life, hidden between

rocks and usually ignored by all except the most curious people. Wildwood State Park, however, does have a considerable population because of a large tent-camping area and trailer camp, so it is a popular weekend retreat and a bit too crowded during summer if you seek a lonely stretch. Plan to walk in Wildwood out of season, when it will be rewarding. It's open all year, dawn to dusk.

To get to Wildwood, take Route 54, Hulse Landing Road, north from Route 25A, Sound Avenue. It is just east of Wading River (631–929–4314). During summer parking is $7.00 daily. Off season it is $5.00 weekends and holidays.

Quite naturally the inland trails are places less frequented, although they are more protected and easier walking than the beach. If it weren't for the trees along the North Shore, erosion would have taken most of Long Island into the sound. So walk here to discover the woodland, the home of numerous insects, birds, and mammals, and bring along a curiosity to get to know still another tree, shrub, or creature with which we share the earth.

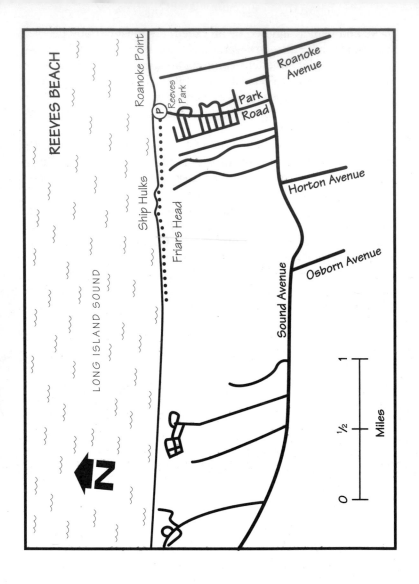

52

Reeves Beach

The town of Riverhead maintains a beach at the end of Roanoke Avenue on Long Island Sound. Off season there is usually no problem parking, though during summer months a permit is required (obtainable at the town recreation department). The bluffs on the sound are extremely high; the beach at the tide line is quite pebbly, has some impressive glacial erratics, and, west just 0.5 mile, is strewn with two ship hulks, wrecks of sometime past. It's a steep walk down to the beach from the parking spot. Turn left and walk a couple of hundred yards, and you will be alone.

For miles along here the border of high wooded bluffs obscures any houses, and there is a feeling of immense loneliness. There are especially wide areas and big tangles of purple beach pea, sea rocket, and bishop's weed. Some reeds at the base of the bluffs are so tall that you can be completely concealed by them. It is nice exploring territory. Tangles of growth conceal old driftwood, and there are wild beach flowers. Fishing offshore here must be pretty good; there are frequently clusters of small boats bobbing not far out and an occasional surfcaster.

We have walked this beach many times, but never during swimming season. Its setting—the beach is tucked down under a high ridge—appeals to us. In a winter rain the Connecticut shoreline is completely obscured. With snow on the frozen ground, you cover distances faster. In early spring we find trailing arbutus on paths up the bluffs, with wintergreen and partridgeberry. The trailing arbutus is particularly satisfying to come upon in blossom—such a delicate fragrance and the tiny, palest lavender petals. On fresh, bright sunny weekends, the promise of a good breeze brings many sails out on the sound, and the clarity lets you see details on the opposite shores. Falling autumn leaves pile up in the gullies, cover paths, and rustle when you pass along. Because we never have any particular objective in mind, we always look at a watch as we start off headed west, and when we remember to look again, we are always surprised by the lateness of the hour. We usually take along field glasses and a camera.

How to get there? Follow Roanoke Avenue north from the Route 58 traffic circle in Riverhead until it ends at Sound Avenue. Then turn left, west, and go a short distance to the second road, Park Road. Turn right, north, and follow up and down a hill or two. The road ends in a modest parking area that overlooks Reeves Beach.

53

Horton Point Park

The Horton Point Lighthouse sits serenely atop a 110-foot bluff, looking something like a canvas by Edward Hopper, over the waters of Long Island Sound facing Connecticut. It was once part of the extensive land allotment of Barnabus Horton, one of the 1640 founders of Southold Town. It is now the chief ornament of a tree-shaded Southold park, which is a beautiful place to picnic. The broad view from this high bluff allegedly led George Washington, a young surveyor from Virginia, to recommend that a navigational light be built here when he passed through in 1757 on his way to Boston. That's a bit of oral history, but the construction in 1857 of the first of a series of more modern lights here is well documented. Today the keeper's house contains an excellent, small marine museum that, like the lighthouse, has been sponsored and improved by the Southold Historical Society.

The eight-acre park provides one of the best seascapes on Long Island's North Shore. Here you can view the sound and visualize its many moods, its past and present commerce and the challenges that faced Long Island refugees traveling to and from the Connecticut coast when eastern Long Island was occupied by the British from 1777 to 1784.

One hundred thirty-two wooden steps take you down to the boulder-strewn beach. In all kinds of weather, it is picturesque because of fisherfolk. They take blackfish from around those rocks. They dig their poles into the sand, light their pipes, and

HORTON POINT PARK

LONG ISLAND SOUND

Lighthouse

Sound View Avenue

Youngs Avenue

25

SOUTHOLD

48

North Road

N

GREAT POND

1

½

0

Miles

keep an eye on the floats, ready to jump and reel in when they bob. We always check to see if they have a few in their pails.

Walking on Horton's beach can be rough because of the pebbles, but it's good for massaging the insteps. Snorkeling is popular here. It's one of the few places on Long Island where we see people in wet suits with scuba tanks and flippers. The huge rocks are relics of the Ice Age.

There is a long beach stretch here to the west that seems uninhabited, very wide with lots of driftwood. And the flotsam that heaves itself up on the beach is fascinating.

Standing on these North Shore bluffs makes Long Island's formation in the geologic past become fundamentally clear. You can imagine the great pushing blade of the glaciers—for geologists say Long Island is wholly the result of the glaciers—shoving a wide, wide swath of sand, soil, rock, and tops of mountains southward like a massive bulldozer and piling it here. Then the ice melted and the waters ran off, washing the soils southward into a plain. The colossal scale of the whole thing can be appreciated when you realize that the ocean was raised to its present level, more than 300 feet higher than it had been, by the melted ice to form Long Island Sound. And what capriciousness there was in shoving and raising the level of the waters can be seen in the structure of peninsulas and spits and tiny islands that make up the shape of the map today.

The force that could bring these huge boulders can be better appreciated when you walk along the beach here, comparing your size to their size. Surely the experience is a universal one, and it is one that will linger with you.

The museum alone is worth a visit if you have any interest in matters nautical or, indeed, local. The collection of scrimshaw, tools, maps, letters, ships' logs and journals, paintings, and more is splendid. You can also climb the tower to inspect the working light and enjoy the view. The museum is normally open on weekends from 11:30 A.M. to 4:00 P.M., between Memorial Day and Columbus Day, but it would be well to check with the historical society in Southold before your visit (631–765–5500 or souhistsoc@aol.com), as special visits can be arranged at other times. There is a suggested donation of $2.00.

A word on getting here. Take the Route 25/48 divided highway (North Road) east from Mattituck until you come to the turnoff for Southold Village (Youngs Avenue). Instead of going right, turn left on Youngs and follow it, past the jog at Sound View Avenue, to the very end.

About the Authors

"We are not hikers—we aren't that goal-oriented." So say the Albrights, trying to make the distinction between walking to get somewhere and walking for fun. For them walking is to look and listen to all the sights and sounds of the woods, the meadows, and the sea.

Priscilla and Rod Albright lived in New York most of their adult lives; having come East to college, they stayed right on. Rod was a television producer for a large advertising agency, and Priscilla served on the boards of several social services agencies.

Now retired, they do their daily walks from three different bases: in summer on an island in the Bay of Fundy where the craggy shores offer some scrambling and the woodland paths are full of birds and blueberries; in fall and spring they walk in the foothills of the White Mountains from a cottage in South Parsonsfield, Maine, near the New Hampshire border; come the depths of winter, a small Airstream trailer goes with them to Florida and Florida trails on pine needles or to the Southwest to walk in canyons or the floor of deserts because they are insatiably curious about the natural world.